HARNESSING
CONFLICT

HOW FAMILY BUSINESSES CAN
SURVIVE AND THRIVE

NICOLE GARTON

Tellwell Talent
www.tellwell.ca

ISBN
978-0-2288-6259-8 (Hardcover)
978-0-2288-6257-4 (Paperback)
978-0-2288-6258-1 (eBook)

CONTENTS

FOREWORD

The fabric of family business is woven from many strands: the hopes and dreams of one generation of a family, the complexity of family dynamics, the stressors of succession from one generation to the next, the conflict styles of the family members, the challenges of identity, hierarchy and passions. With approximately 80% of Canadian businesses family run, the health of these businesses is not only important for the families involved, but also important for the overarching Canadian economy.

Nicole Garton's book, ***Harnessing Conflict***, *How Family Businesses can Survive and Thrive* is aptly titled, as it explores the ambitious goal of conflict transformation in family business. Garton grabs our attention at the beginning with the narrative of a wealthy Canadian family mired in litigation over the family enterprise. She carefully traces the narrative arc of this family; the first generation rags to riches story, the mentoring and support of the second generation into the business, and then the seemingly unavoidable conflicts surging into the maelstrom that rips the relationships apart and threatens the health of the business enterprises.

Garton then skilfully dissects the elements and causes of conflict, particularly as they relate to family business. She makes conflict theory accessible and relatable, and takes the reader through the dynamics of conflict as these dynamics impact family business.

She then moves the reader through specifics aimed at conflict prevention and resolution. But she does not stop there. As she explains, conflict is a signal that transformation is urgently needed. She steps beyond the field of conflict resolution to explore the importance of conflict transformation. As she points out, resolution can be a way of avoiding change, and when change is needed, conflict transformation is the necessary work to be done.

While conflict resolution can be difficult, conflict transformation can present an even greater challenge. For family businesses, the welcome news is that this slim volume is packed with information to help family businesses create and sustain health. Garton has obviously not only studied conflict theories in depth, but also clearly understands and is able to synthesize these theories. She uses her detailed understanding to explain these theories in a way that can be understood and applied. ***Harnessing Conflict*** is one of those books that will be well-thumbed, not only for the distillation of conflict theory but also for the practical suggestions for building family business health. ***Harnessing Conflict*** is an important contribution that should find a place in the offices of all family businesses, and in the libraries of all professionals who support family enterprises.

Nancy Cameron, Q.C.
Author of *Collaborative Practice: Deepening the Dialogue*

CHAPTER 1

A MOTOR OF CHANGE

"Happy families are all alike; every unhappy family is unhappy in its own way." So begins Count Leo Tolstoy's 1877 novel *Anna Karenina*. Several generations of readers have mused over the meaning of this sentence. I suspect Tolstoy was assuming that "happy" families are the norm, the baseline, the rule rather than the exception. Their members enjoy good health, have an acceptable level of financial well-being, and are bound by mutual self-interest and affection. These things do not make for conflict and, therefore, do not make for an interesting novel, let alone one in excess of 340,000 words. Since most families don't attract much attention, and therefore don't become fodder for novels, tell-all memoirs, or tabloid headlines, we assume they enjoy a kind of homeostasis—a state of being without serious conflict—are therefore happy, and in their happiness, are indistinguishable from most other families.

We assume we know what makes for happiness. In a word, it is satisfaction, which many would define as the absence of conflict. But we know less about precisely what makes for an unhappy family, and when we encounter one we therefore find ourselves quite intrigued. We find ourselves in the presence of the exception, and the human brain is hardwired to pay close attention to the exceptional.

Beginning in 2018, Canadians were riveted by the "Stronach Family Feud," which exploded into a massive lawsuit filed by family patriarch Frank Stronach and his wife Elfriede against their daughter Belinda, their grandchildren Nicole and Frankie, and Stronach Group CEO Alon Ossip for allegedly misappropriating the funds of the family business. At stake in the suit was more than half a billion Canadian dollars. Unsurprisingly, it triggered a tangle of countersuits and counterclaims from other family members.

The early story of Frank Stronach is a classic tale of rags-to-riches. Born Franz Strohsack to working-class parents in 1932, the nadir of Great Depression in Austria, the youngster came of age during a time of economic hardship, followed immediately by World War II. When he was 14, he dropped out of school to apprentice as a tool and die maker. Eight years later, in 1954, he immigrated to Montreal, Quebec, and later moved to Ontario. In Canada, he married a fellow Austrian Elfriede Sallmutter and by 1956 had sprinted forward by rapid bounds from apprentice to tool and die maker to entrepreneur, starting his first business, Multimatic Investments Ltd., in Toronto. Thirteen years later, Multimatic won its first automotive parts contract and merged with Magna Electronics. In 1973, Stronach changed the name of his company to the resoundingly regal Magna International Ltd.

Based in Aurora, Ontario, Magna International became a major international automotive parts enterprise. It spawned Magna Europa, headquartered in Austria, which, in 1998, took over Steyr-Daimler-Puch, a major manufacturing conglomerate. Two years later, Magna International created the Magna Entertainment Corporation as a separate public company, which subsequently filed for Chapter 11 bankruptcy. Frank then created a new entity, the Stronach Group, which purchased Magna Entertainment's holding and became an entertainment and real estate company focused mainly on two of Frank's passions, thoroughbred horse racing and pari-mutuel wagering. Today, the Stronach Group (doing business as 1/ST) owns several iconic racetracks including Santa Anita in California, Gulfstream in Florida, Golden Gate Fields in California, and Pimlico, Laurel Park, and Rosecroft, all in Maryland.

So, what went wrong? How did the conduct of this complex and varied family business create a broad, bitter, and apparently unbridgeable chasm dividing father from daughter and, within the family, the allies of both?

Dan Donovan, who served four years as vice-president of corporate affairs for Magna International, recalled how Stronach and his daughter were always together. Frank was the poor kid made good, ever willing to take extravagant business risks, and Belinda was the princess born into her father's wealth. Frank's financial success made them very different, and yet—call it DNA, call it learning by example—they were also very much alike. Both were workaholics, competitive, hard-driven. Donovan described them as "both very determined people ... uncompromising on certain things, in their own ways." He found "irony" in the lawsuit because it was such a situation of "like father like daughter."[1]

The fact is that Frank Stronach "spent decades grooming his daughter ... to take over his billion-dollar business"[2] then, suddenly, he wanted it all back.

Extreme as the Stronach family business battle is, it tells us a great deal about the nature of all family business conflict, and we'll get further into the details as this book progresses. For now, it is sufficient to tell enough of the story to appreciate the magnitude of the battle, a fight for control of the Stronach Group, of which Belinda Stronach has now become CEO and President.

Filed in the Ontario Superior Court of Justice (Commercial List) on October 1, 2018, Frank Stronach's Statement of Claim against his daughter and Alon Ossip runs to 73 "excoriating" pages that boil down to the accusation that Belinda and Ossip "defrauded him to gain control of the family fortune." As Leah McLaren wrote in *Toronto Life*, the document "burns with explosive patriarchal rage, concluding with Frank's demand that Belinda and Ossip be removed as trustees of the family trust."[3]

Before we examine the frayed strands of this tangled conflict in some detail, let's try to find its essence, what lawyers call its *gravamen*.

Frank Stronach "groomed" his daughter to succeed him. She was not, however, a "spoiled" or "entitled" family member. She showed early promise and grew into an extraordinarily accomplished woman. She was a member of Canada's House of Commons from 2004 to 2008 and served as Minister of Human Resources and Skills Development and Minister Responsible for Democratic Renewal in the government of Paul Martin. When she left politics in 2008, she became vice chairman of Magna International, which was Canada's largest automotive parts maker. She held this post until December 31, 2010, when she became chairman and president of the Stronach Group.

Magna was a publicly traded company, whereas the Stronach Group was privately held. Inasmuch as Frank Stronach founded both and Belinda Stronach served in lofty executive positions in both, they could certainly be described as family businesses. Yet their extent and governance reached well beyond the family. That is why the bitter language of the "patriarch's" Statement of Claim is so striking. He focused the dispute on a fight for control, not only of a set of companies, but of the *family's* fortune.

That fortune is symbolized by the sprawling Stronach family compound in Aurora, a spread that includes the Stronach Group headquarters along with three family mansions (one for Frank and Elfriede, one for Belinda and her children, and one for Frank's only son, Andrew, and his family), a golf course, and an artificial lake. Literally, there was no separation between company and family.

Startled by the vitriol of Frank's claim, friends of the family nevertheless believed that Frank intended it as nothing more than a shot across his daughter's bow. But she responded with a counterclaim that was equally vitriolic, and hurled back upon her father the very charges he leveled against her: reckless spending, incompetent leadership, and blatant fraud.

Belinda was born in 1966 and her brother Andrew two years later. As a son, Andrew would likely have been the conventional choice as apparent to the family businesses, but Frank clearly saw that his daughter had a drive and a charisma similar to his own, whereas Andrew was not (Frank thought) cut out to be a business leader. He therefore focused on his daughter, letting Andrew go his own way—which, it turned out, was cattle ranching, an interest Frank himself would pursue with reckless abandon.

Belinda was an athlete, popular, and a self-driven hard-worker. She was constantly at her father's side and Frank clearly adored her. When she turned 16, he gave her a silver Camaro Z-28, which was a special-edition Indy pace car. Belinda studied business at New York University but dropped out after her freshman year to work in the family business. When she was 22, Frank appointed her to the board of directors. After all, he himself had left school at age 14. Belinda rose through the Magna ranks from vice-president to executive vice-president. In 1992, the company went public and in 2000 was named by *Forbes* as the world's top auto parts company.

While Frank Stronach continued to present the public face of a scrappy immigrant entrepreneur turned savvy tycoon, in private he increasingly acted the overbearing patriarch. "If you went out to dinner with Frank," an associate recalled, "he would tell you where to sit and what to eat. And he meant it."[4]

He had built a great business on a homely product: auto parts. Having been spectacularly successful at that, he increasingly turned over Magna International operations to Belinda while he shifted his focus from projects justified in terms of business, to projects justified by nothing more (or less) than his own passions. He planned to build World of Wonder, a theme park on the outskirts of Vienna, and he started Magna Air, a transatlantic luxury airline. Neither the park nor the airline got off the ground.

That is when he created Magna Entertainment Corporation ("MEC") for the purpose of buying and developing racetracks. Almost overnight, MEC became the largest owner-operator of thoroughbred tracks in North America. Shareholders who had invested in a successful auto parts manufacturer were shocked to discover that their money had bought Santa Anita in 1998 for US$126 million.

It was at about this same time that Frank built the combination family compound and corporate headquarters in Aurora and began thinking seriously about succession. He had carefully crafted a Stronach family trust and assigned to it his Magna voting shares. He installed himself as super-trustee, empowered to appoint and remove all other trustees at will. These maneuvers executed, he named Belinda Magna CEO of Magna International in 2001.

Despite her father's extravagance, Belinda helmed Magna International successfully before stunning the Canadian business community by stepping down from Magna in 2004 to enter politics. Running as a Conservative, she won a seat in Parliament that same year and in 2005 made headlines again by crossing the floor into Prime Minister Paul Martin's Liberal cabinet. But as the Liberal Party faltered in 2006, she returned to Magna International, which was continuing to prosper.

It was during the interval of Belinda' absence from Magna that Frank befriended Alon Ossip. A tax lawyer by profession, Ossip was strikingly different from Frank Stronach. He was soft-spoken where Stronach was loud, and detail oriented where Stronach was impulsive. As if to prove the maxim that opposites attract, Frank hired him as executive vice-president at Magna. It was a good choice, as he soon proved indispensable in leading Magna to even greater success. The result, Leah McLaren wrote in *Toronto Life*, was that Alon Ossip "became bound as tightly to Frank and Belinda by money as they are by blood."[5]

Blood and money. These are the alpha and omega of conflict in family business.

In the meantime, the patriarch persisted in throwing cash into ill-advised passion projects, including an electric bike company and an energy drink branded with an Austrian theme. Neither advanced. Another side of Frank was exhibited in a bold act of charity: the construction of a modular housing development in Louisiana for 300 survivors of Hurricane Katrina. Yet even this was tinged with grandiosity, as Stronach christened it Magnaville.

He doubled down on his enduring enthusiasm for thoroughbred breeding and racing by expanding into cattle raising. In 2010, Stronach purchased 90,000 acres in Ocala, Florida and founded Adena Farms, which he planned to transform into an all-natural, grass-fed cattle farm and beef processing operation. Over the next half-dozen years, the Stronachs poured some US$300 million into Adena. To the breeding and processing operations there, Frank added a members-only golf and country club, around which he planned to develop a luxury residential community. He also opened two restaurants—and projected a chain of specialty stores dedicated to carrying Adena Farms beef. While driving one day, Frank encountered a grove of oaks miles down the road from Adena. It triggered a brainstorm. He would acquire the site and create a separate organic hog farm to produce acorn-fed pork. That the hog farm was located too far from Adena to use the same meat-processing plant was no obstacle. Frank decided to build a second plant. On its own however, Adena quickly became a money pit. Ocala was wonderful horse country but lacked the proper soil to produce grass-fed cattle. Building the hog farm so far from the original Adena site—based solely on the fact that it was rich in oaks and Frank wanted to feed acorns to the pigs—was a staggeringly unnecessary additional expense.

Clearly, Frank Stronach had stopped making business decisions. Instead, he used his track record of business success to justify the execution of passions, dreams, and whims without the benefit of research or independent advice. Symbolically, in 2012, he commissioned a 12-story, 110-foot-high statue of the mythical flying horse Pegasus slaying a fire-breathing dragon as part of an entertainment and retail attraction adjacent to his thoroughbred racetrack and casino at Hallendale Beach, Florida.[6]

The sculpture, which was based on Stronach's own sketches, was intended for Pegasus Park, another projected amusement park, roller-coaster included. The plan was to put a 5-D theatre *inside* Pegasus. Thanks to Belinda's intervention, the park was never built and the sculpture, sans internal theatre, was repurposed for Hallendale. It was one of two bronze castings of the sculpture made in a Chinese foundry, the other has never left storage in China. The projected price for these creations was US$6 million. In the end, they came in overbudget at US$55 million.

The Pegasus episode came two years after Frank stunned the Canadian business community in May 2010 by giving up his majority Magna shareholder voting rights in a deal valued at $983 million. In 2011, acting on Frank's instructions, Ossip structured an additional $700 million deal to swap the rest of the family's voting rights for Magna's horse racing and gaming assets. This was the foundation of the Stronach Group, which was created as a trust to manage the Stronach family wealth by distributing it across four business divisions: racetracks and gaming; real estate development; agriculture; and breeding, training, and racing. For his labour on the deal, Ossip received a 5% interest in Stronach Group assets not included in the family trust. Belinda was appointed chair and president of the newly created group, and she (with Frank's support) named Ossip as CEO.

With her father's blessing, Belinda Stronach was now the public face of the Stronach family's businesses. She lacked her father's passion for racing, but she was determined to lift the family's interests by taking action to reverse the ongoing decline of thoroughbred racing in North America. She obtained high-profile celebrity endorsements and participation in the racetracks, and she introduced a series of much-needed health and safety reforms into the racing industry. The Group's racing and gaming sales nearly doubled through 2017 during her leadership.

Instead of celebrating his daughter's successful stewardship, Frank Stronach seemed to resent it, expressing his resentment by pouring more Stronach Group resources into Adena Farms. At Belinda's direction, Ossip tried to talk him down. Frank responded by attempting to co-opt Ossip but this only drove Ossip further into Belinda's camp.

In the meantime, in 2012, Frank entered politics—*Austrian* politics—founding a party called Team Stronach, financed by the Stronach Group. Frank and his party's slate won 11 parliamentary seats, and it was only afterward that Frank discovered he was obliged by Austrian tax law to make extensive financial disclosures. This prompted him, in 2013, to resign from all corporate positions in the Stronach Group, including his position as super-trustee. He appointed Belinda to the positions he had vacated, and Ossip, as well as Belinda's two children, were added as trustees.

By this point, the Stronach story was about to explode into a full-dress Shakespearean tragedy – *King Lear* comes to mind. All that was required was a spark to ignite the powder packed into the keg.

That came in the form of a set of undated documents, drawn up by the Stronach Group's attorneys, announcing the resignation of Belinda's children as trustees and the reappointment of Frank Stronach Sr. Under legal challenge, Frank later claimed that he had requested the documents to enable his self-reappointment as super-trustee. Both Belinda and Ossip contradicted this, pointing out that if the documents had been instigated by Frank, it would be a blatantly illegal ruse to avoid Austrian legal requirements for income and wealth disclosure. Belinda asserted that the documents had been created at Ossip's insistence out of concern that Belinda's two children would be his only co-trustees in the event of Belinda's death or incapacity (she was a breast cancer survivor).

For his part, Frank quickly grew impatient with Austrian politics and, in January 2014, plunged back into Adena Farms, expanding the operation and pouring into it yet more proceeds from the sale of Stronach Group assets. He did this, he said, on the understanding that the reappointment documents had already taken effect, and he accused Belinda and Ossip of complicity in creating this understanding. In short, *they* tricked him into believing that he possessed authority that he no longer had. Denying any such deception, Belinda and Ossip argued categorically that Frank had largely withdrawn from the family business and that he had now used his purported "delusion" as a perverse maneuver to resume control.

We can clearly see that the conflict built up over years. In part, it was the result of Frank Stronach's inability or unwillingness to separate his patriarchal position in the family from his leadership position in the family's businesses. In part, it was also due to his failure or inability to separate his paternal love for his daughter from his apparently amply merited confidence in her as a businessperson. He was also unable to deal adequately with feelings that his daughter, whom he had groomed as his successor, had succeeded perhaps *too* well, so that he came to perceive her as a competitor. Finally, as he grew older, Frank had begun making increasingly outlandish business decisions that proved very costly.

The issue of the reappointment documents served as a catalyst that transformed the conflict from a family fight and business dispute, into a legal battle involving both the family's wealth and the conduct of its business. The wall that should have divided the realms of business and family simply crumbled.

Frank opened Adena Golf and Country Club in Florida in 2015, the same year that Belinda established, on her own, Acasta Enterprises, an acquisition company. The irony here is that both Adena and Acasta were losers. But Ossip pointed out that the patriarch's projects had already taken $800 million from the family's net worth. He warned Frank that the Stronach Group was facing liquidity issues. When Frank resisted, Ossip told him to talk to his daughter. With this, Belinda warned her father that she would stop him from attempting to act on behalf of the business. Her father shot back with an order to fire Ossip, whom he blamed for setting them against one another. Belinda compromised by suspending Ossip from the business until the dispute had cooled.

The maneuver bought a brief respite over the Christmas holidays. Come New Year however, the fight was on again. Frank Stronach dated the hitherto undated reappointment documents and informed Belinda that he had reappointed himself as a trustee. Belinda responded in writing that she refused to allow him to take control of the business. With that, the two began a mediation and came to an agreement to fund, through the Stronach Group, capital and operating expenditures for Adena Farms for the next three years to a maximum of US$40 million. Frank was named chair of Adena Farms and given signing authority over farm expenditures under $1 million.

This ephemeral truce was over before the month was up, as Frank forged ahead with plans for Adena that greatly exceeded the budget. Belinda responded by cancelling the leases for Adena's proposed retail operation and fired employees without her father's knowledge. With that, she summarily assumed control over Adena, closing down the golf course and putting the land up at a fire-sale price. In court papers, she later alleged that her father bullied her children into signing documents reappointing him as trustee.

She further claimed that he meddled with company boards and blocked her access to certain bank funds.

Now the larger immediate family did what many families do in this situation. They chose sides. Elfriede sided with her husband, as did Belinda's brother, Andrew, and Andrew's daughter, Selena. They argued that Belinda prioritized her own financial interests over those of the Stronach Group. Belinda responded that she was only doing her fiduciary duty to protect the family fortune.

Christmas 2017 was very different from Christmas 2016. There was no truce, and the family factions went their separate ways for the holiday. Depressed by what was happening to the family, Belinda proposed splitting family assets based on the current equity interests in the family trust and the family businesses. This would give Belinda and her children the racing and gaming businesses; while Andrew, Selena, and Elfriede would get the non-racing and non-gaming assets, including the agriculture group. Belinda would also make a cash payout to Andrew.

None of the family responded to her proposal. A stalemate ensued—until Belinda sold the company jet. In any other family and family business, this sale would have been a small matter within an apocalyptic context. For Frank Stronach, however, it was the proverbial last straw. He brought his headline-making suit against Ossip, Belinda, and her children, seeking to regain control of the family businesses. Shortly after this, Andrew sued Belinda, supporting his father's reinstatement as trustee. Belinda filed a long and unsparing counterclaim. Andrew's wife, Kathleen, filed for divorce—apparently seeking to secure financial support prior to the outcome of the suit. And before the year ended, Selena, 18 years old, sued Belinda.

Reading even a brief summary of the Stronach saga, one could be forgiven for making two assumptions. First: Family businesses are fraught with peril and are best avoided; at the very least, families should sell their businesses and each family member invest the proceeds from the sale as best they can—individually. Second: Conflict within a family and conflict within a business are both bad; conflict in a family business is even worse. In all cases, conflict should be avoided.

The first assumption, understandable as it is, obscures a far more nuanced truth. The fact is that family ownership of an enterprise offers at least as many opportunities for financial and emotional gain as it does for financial and emotional loss. Families are bound by blood, by affection, and by many areas of collective self-interest, including the desire to create a family legacy; to preserve, perpetuate, and advance the family through time; and to be part of a family that has a positive impact on the world.

These shared desires are opportunities, great opportunities, profound opportunities, though, it is true, they don't come without risks. Yet what business opportunity—with or without family ownership—comes without risk? Since business is at bottom an exchange of value for value, there can be no reward without risk.

Whether or not these arguments persuade you, they have persuaded the majority of those who start, run, and lead businesses. In Canada, some 8 out of 10 businesses are family-run. The most successful of these make an impact far beyond the families that create them, run them, and sometimes sell them. The fraction of family-run Canadian businesses that drive the wealth of Canadian very-high-net-worth and ultra-high-net-worth families is significant. This means that the future prosperity and value of some of Canada's most prominent businesses are bound up with the future prosperity and value of the families who own them.

While common sense may suggest that the family business is inherently selfish—run exclusively by the family solely for the benefit of the family, this is not the case. The wealthiest families in Canada, and most everywhere else, do not live, work, and earn exclusively for themselves. Most look toward the future, the rising generation of their family as well as the generations yet unborn. Most also look toward the future of the business or businesses they have built and may yet build, businesses they may grow and run, businesses they may pass down through the family, and businesses they may sell to other individuals or corporate entities. Families who create significant enterprises are concerned with how these enterprises will contribute to the economy of Canada, the continent, and often, the whole world. They are anxious to ensure that their entrepreneurial investments, in real estate, in venture capital, in new business start-ups, will positively impact their fellow Canadians and their fellow human beings. Most high-net-worth families are also committed to devoting a large fraction of their wealth directly to philanthropic projects and causes, which are often initiatives that they don't merely fund, but establish, build, and lead. As taken as Frank Stronach was with self-absorbed "passion" projects, he also built a development of 300 modular homes for victims of Hurricane Katrina. It was no small undertaking.

As for the second possible takeaway from the Stronach story, that conflict is bad and to be avoided at all costs, we need only consider that most major endeavours are not begun on a note of concord but on one of disagreement, if not outright conflict. If everyone is thinking alike, an old saying goes, nobody is thinking. If you need a higher authority than such homespun leadership wisdom, look to the great nineteenth-century German philosopher Georg Wilhelm Fredrich Hegel. The dialectic—discourse between two or more people with conflicting points of view who wish to advance beyond conflict and come to the truth—is the simple heart and soul of his philosophy. Individuals, organizations, and civilizations, he argued, make progress through dialectic—in other words, through conflict. You propose a *thesis,* the statement of an idea or point of view; I propose an *antithesis*, a reaction that contradicts or even negates your thesis. Stop here, and we are stalemated in conflict. Hegel proposes a third step: *synthesis.* This is a formulation or statement through which the conflict created by *thesis* confronting *antithesis* is resolved—as a new truth, a new method, a more productive and inclusive way of seeing and doing something.

John Paul Lederach holds the unique title of Professor of International Peacebuilding at the University of Notre Dame (Notre Dame, Indiana) and is the founding director for the Center for Justice and Peacebuilding at Eastern Mennonite University, where he is also a professor. His *Little Book of Conflict Transformation* is a classic—not on "resolving" conflict but on *transforming* it. The idea of a dialectic is not to let *thesis* and *antithesis* fight it out until only one of them is left standing, (which also leaves the possibility that both may be annihilated!) rather, it is to let the two engage in conflict until a new entity, *synthesis*, is produced. In other words, the best thing to do with conflict is neither to extinguish its flames nor fan them into all-engulfing conflagration. It is to transform the conflict into something new, better and more productive than either side of the conflict offers.

Conflict transformation is constructive change. As Lederach writes, "Conflict is normal in human relationships, and conflict is a motor of change."[7]

If conflict is "normal," it cannot be avoided. If conflict is a motor of change, it should not be avoided—not in a family, not in a business, and not in a family business. Conflict happens for a reason or a set of reasons. Merely "resolving" a conflict rarely gets to the topic at the heart of the conflict, which is usually an issue of welfare or justice or some other form of disputed equity. Does anyone think that covering up such issues is a viable way of dealing with conflict? In fact, resolution is a way of avoiding change—evading transformation in precisely the kind of situation where transformation is most urgently called for.

Let's redefine conflict this way: *Conflict is a signal that transformation is urgently needed.* That is why conflict is a motor of change. As Lederach explains it:

Transformation provides a clear and important vision because it brings into focus the horizon toward which we journey—the building of healthy relationships and communities, locally and globally. This goal requires real change in our current ways of relating.[8]

The takeaway is that transformation and the benefits it brings—to families, businesses, and family businesses—cannot begin until it becomes a goal, and it cannot become a goal until conflict provides the urgent need for transformation.

This book is about conflict in family businesses. Far more important, it is about the transformation of conflict in family businesses. Its goal is not to tell the reader how to suppress conflict, avoid conflict, detour around conflict, or get beyond conflict. Its goal is to show how conflict may be harnessed as a creative motor of change and evolution.

How do you know when change is needed? Easy. You are suddenly confronted with, or about to be engulfed by, *conflict*.

CHAPTER 2

THE DYNAMICS
OF CONFLICT

"Conflict," John Paul Lederach writes in *The Little Book of Conflict Transformation,* "flows from life."[9] As long as we are alive, we cannot escape life, so, it stands to reason, we cannot escape conflict. Moreover, since nothing with which we, as individuals, are associated brings us closer to life than family, family will not allow us to escape conflict. Add to this the fact that business inevitably creates situations of conflict, and we may conclude that the family business is a veritable petri dish for the growth of conflict.

Such authorities on conflict as John W. Budd, Alexander J. S. Colvin, and Dionne Pohler conclude that conflict, defined as an apparent or latent opposition between two or more parties that results from differences that are either real or imagined, is an inevitable part of human interaction. However, Lederach adds that, properly managed, conflict can be understood as "providing opportunities to grow and to increase understanding of ourselves, of others, of our social structures. Conflicts in relationships at all levels are the way life helps us to stop, assess, and take notice. ... [T]hrough conflict we respond, innovate, and change. ... Conflict ... keeps relationships and social structures honest, alive, and dynamically responsive to human needs, aspirations, and growth."[10]

But, let's admit it, conflict *itself* begins much closer to what Budd, Colvin, and Pohler describe than to the *transformation* of conflict that Lederach outlines. It begins where one party perceives that another party has negatively affected, or is about to negatively affect, something that the first party cares about. And it manifests itself in incompatibility, disagreement, or dissonance within groups, organizations, businesses, families, or some combination of these.[11]

Understanding Conflict

Common sense and tradition tell us that conflict arises from opposing interests involving scarce resources, divergence in setting goals, and frustration and anger resulting from either of these circumstances. While scarcity of resources varies from situation to situation, business to business, and family to family, we might assume that in situations of plenty, the chances of conflict are less. This ignores, however, the most basic assumption of economics, the Law of Scarcity, which states that no economic resource— land, capital, labour, talent—is infinite. This means that not everyone can have everything they want. No wonder Thomas Carlyle branded economics "the dismal science." The Law of Scarcity ensures that at least one thing will always be available in plentiful supply: causes for conflict. Moreover, because resources are finite and desires potentially infinite, conflict typically reflects the assumption that the struggle for resolution is inherently and at bottom a zero-sum game. For one side to win, the other must lose.[12]

There is another approach to conflict, which is to understand it as a dynamic process. Again, both common sense and tradition tend to drive us toward thinking about the ultimate expression of conflict as a showdown. No doubt, some conflicts do culminate in a "nuclear option"— dissolution of a partnership, a project, or a company. Some conflicts really do end with only one person left standing. Legends of the Wild West are full of conflicts "settled" in just such a way at high noon. But in the real world, such zero-sum Armageddons are relatively uncommon. More often, a conflict is less an event than it is a relationship; a relationship between two or more individuals that can be analyzed as a sequence of conflict episodes. Each episode is certainly capable of creating destructive escalation, but each also offers the possibility of producing alternative, more cooperative courses of development.[13] Some of these alternatives may even be what Lederach calls "transformative," redirecting the potentially destructive flow of anger and discontent into a powerful cataract capable of driving constructive energy.

Situations of conflict can be noisy, and therefore appear chaotic. In fact, conflict typically comes in four main forms.

Intrapersonal conflict is experienced by a single individual when their own goals, values, or roles diverge internally. In such cases, the individual becomes "conflicted." Often, the internal conflict is associated with cognitive dissonance, a state in which the individual holds contradictory beliefs, values, or ideas. This can create a level of anxiety, which can rise to genuine crisis when a person is driven by one belief or idea to take or participate in an action that goes against their other contradictory values.

Interpersonal conflict results from differences between two or more people who are required to interact.

Intragroup conflict is **interpersonal conflict** within a group or team.

Intergroup conflict pits groups or teams against one another. Such conflict can arise between two (or more) groups within the same organization.

Within all these conflict types (except intrapersonal conflict), the conflict may be *horizontal*, that is, conflict among individuals at the same peer level, or it may be *vertical*, conflict between a subordinate and a superior.

In understanding conflict, it may also be useful to distinguish between substantive conflict (often referred to as "task and process" conflict) and relationship conflict. Substantive and relationship conflict can occur independently of each other, one type of conflict can turn into another, or they can occur simultaneously.[14]

In the category of substantive conflict, task conflict involves tensions and disagreements on the nature of tasks individuals work on. The conflict is manifested in contradicting opinions and views about goals and technical issues relating to the tasks at hand. Moderate levels of task conflict often improve decision-making. Effective decision-makers routinely go out of their way to seek a range of opinions. In other words, they leverage moderate task conflict to arrive at the best solution among several options. This is a common example of the positive power of conflict, including in the family business. Like any other form of conflict, however, task conflict can become destructively heated.

Process conflict, which is disagreement about *how* work should be accomplished (and which may include disagreements about the organization of work, plans, timetables, and so on), resembles task conflict in that moderate levels often help in sharing and transferring the knowledge by which groups, including the family business, can innovate and improve efficiency and performance.[15]

Relationship conflict deals with interpersonal tensions between individuals caused by their relationship and not by the tasks or processes they perform. Relationship conflict can result in anger, distrust, animosity, and rivalry among coworkers. When these coworkers also happen to be family members, the intensity of the conflict can be expected to increase. In contrast to substantive conflict, which can be quite productive when the degree of conflict is moderate, there is rarely any upside to relationship conflict. Rather, it interferes with the conduct of business and degrades the goodwill and mutual understanding among a group or among family members. When relationship conflict is chronic in a family business, the firm's performance can be expected to suffer. Relationship conflict therefore cries out for resolution.[16]

Understanding How Conflicts Develop

Conflicts, then, are not necessarily sudden showdown explosions. Often, especially in organizations and families, they develop sequentially. Students of conflict refer to the sequential process as a spiral, or escalation ladder of conflict:

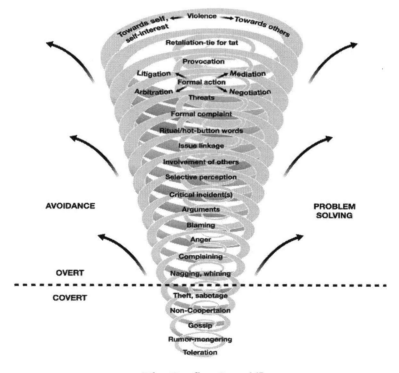

The Conflict Spiral.[17]

Of course, not every conflict follows this escalation exactly. Some phases may be skipped or occur in different orders, and some phases may be different from those presented here.

The spiral is designed to suggest a tornado. The more a conflict progresses up the spiral, the stronger the effect of the conflict and the more difficult it is to get out of. The spiral is divided into two zones, the covert and the overt. The covert zone is where the conflict has not yet emerged into public view, and the overt zone is where the conflict becomes public and direct.

While, as I have just noted, it can be difficult to extricate oneself from the spiral, there are multiple strategies available to do so at each stage, and we will discuss these later in the book.

The tornadic spiral is an evocative representation of sequential conflict, but some may prefer a simpler analytical breakdown into just five discrete stages: potential opposition or incompatibility; cognition and personalization; intentions; behaviour; and outcomes.

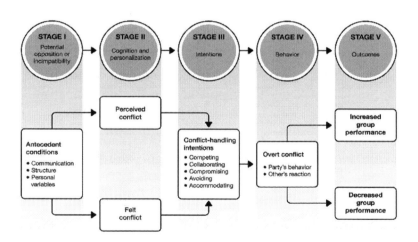

The Conflict Process.[18]

The first stage in the conflict process is **potential opposition or incompatibility**: conditions that are conducive to the creation of conflict. Such conditions are necessary but not inherently sufficient to generate conflict. That is, these conditions do not always lead to conflict, but one or more of them must be present if conflict is to occur. Three general categories, or "antecedent conditions," make up this stage:

1. Communication
2. Structure
3. Personal variables

Miscommunication and ambiguity are frequent sources of conflict, as is too much or too little communication. Too much communication can be overwhelming and confusing, while too little can create frustration over lack of information or connection.

The structure of a group can be a second cause for conflict. "Structure" includes size (larger groups increase the probability of conflict), degree of specialization (more specialized activity within the group increases the probability of conflict), jurisdictional clarity (ambiguity in the allocation of responsibility and roles increases the probability of conflict), goal incompatibility (difference of goals among group members increases the probability of conflict), leadership style differences, dependence (interdependence triggers conflict), and remuneration systems (conflict is caused whenever resources are thought to be distributed unfairly).[19]

Personal variables are the third major antecedent to conflict. These are exceedingly variable, ranging from the mere sound of another person's voice, to facial expressions, to personality, values, or other traits and characteristics.

The second stage of conflict is **cognition and personalization.** Conflict does not exist unless a party perceives (whether accurately or not) the presence of antecedent conditions. At this second stage, conflict issues are defined and parties make conclusions as to what the conflict is about. Whether the conflict is viewed negatively or positively contributes to how it is dealt with and what its outcome will be. Emotions play a major role in the perception of a conflict. If negative emotions are present, trust erodes and negative interpretations of the other party's behaviour proliferate. If positive emotions are present, creative, innovative, and even transformational conflict resolution options are typically considered as, at least, possible.[20]

The third stage in the conflict process consists of a party's **intentions** to act in a certain way. One party must infer the other party's intention to decide how to respond to that party's behaviour. Many conflicts escalate simply because one party attributes the wrong (that is, unintended) intentions to the other. There is also often incongruity between intentions and behaviour, so behaviour does not always accurately reflect a party's intentions.

There are five primary conflict-handling intentions:

1. Competing (assertive and uncooperative)
2. Collaborating (assertive and cooperative)
3. Avoiding (unassertive and uncooperative)
4. Accommodating (unassertive and cooperative)
5. Compromising (midrange on both assertiveness and cooperativeness)

We will review conflict-handling intentions in more detail later in this book.

The fourth stage in the conflict process is **behaviour**. As in the conflict spiral, it is at the overt behavioural stage that conflict becomes visible to others. Conflict behaviours may include statements, actions, and reactions as the parties act out their intentions through a dynamic process of interaction. Behaviour may deviate from a party's original intentions because of unwarranted assumptions, misapprehensions, miscalculations, confusion, or other errors.

The Conflict-Intensity Continuum provides a way of visualizing conflict behaviour:

CONFLICT-INTENSITY CONTINUUM

Annihilatory conflict

- Overt efforts to destroy the other party
- Aggressive physical attacks
- Threats and ultimatums
- Assertive verbal attacks
- Overt questioning or challenging of other
- Minor disagreements or misunderstandings

No conflict

The Conflict-Intensity Continuum.[21]

All conflicts exist somewhere along this continuum, ranging from no conflict to efforts at annihilation. In the lower part of the continuum, controlled forms of functional conflict take place, while on the upper part, increasingly dysfunctional conflict ensues, accompanied by increasingly aggressive (and destructive) action.

The final stage in the conflict process is the **outcome** or consequence. Functional outcomes of conflict may be positive, such as improving the quality of decision making, stimulating creativity and innovation, and encouraging interest and curiosity among parties. These positive developments may result in providing a mechanism through which problems can be aired and tensions released, and an environment of self-evaluation and change may be fostered or created.

On the other hand, of course, dysfunctional conflicts result in a degradation of the effectiveness of a group, a business, a family, or a family business. Among the undesirable consequences of conflict on a family business are poor communication, reduced trust between parties, reductions in the company's cohesiveness, and the subordination of business goals to the primacy of infighting between parties. At the extreme, conflict can bring the operations of the business to a halt, and even threaten its survival. Many researchers theorize that conflict is a major contributor to the often cited statistics on the frequent failure of succession in family businesses.

Sources of Conflict

Human needs are at the core of all conflicts. People engage in conflict because they have needs that they believe can be attained only through conflict or that are directly satisfied by the conflict process itself. These human needs are expressed through other proximate causes: history, structure or context, emotions, values, and communication. Human needs and the proximate causes of conflict are illustrated in Bernard Mayer's Wheel of Conflict:[22]

The Wheel of Conflict

Attempts to understand a conflict should start by examining the proximate causes. By understanding the conflict's history and structure, as well as the emotions, values, and communication involved, you may derive a more detailed understanding of the deeper human needs of the parties to a conflict. These needs range from survival to substantive, procedural, and psychological needs, to identity-based needs for community, meaning, intimacy, and autonomy.

The **structure** or context within which a conflict takes place can contribute to a conflict, including available resources, decision-making procedures, time constraints, legal requirements, communication mechanisms, and physical setting. For example, the litigation process is a structure that can enormously exacerbate conflict by making compromise more difficult and casting issues into irreconcilable right-versus-wrong and win-versus-lose oppositions.

Emotions fuel conflict. Emotions can be generated by the interactions of the conflict, the circumstances surrounding the conflict, or by previous experiences. While emotions can fuel conflict, they can also play a key role in de-escalating conflict. After all, at some level, we all share the desire for connection, affirmation, and acceptance.

The **history** of participants in a conflict or in the system in which the conflict occurs exerts a powerful influence on the course of the conflict. The relationships and past experiences shared by the parties to the conflict can lead them to make both positive and negative assumptions about one another. Rather than operate on assumptions, it is far better to speak to one another. But clear **communication** can be a challenge, especially in emotionally charged circumstances. Conflict, therefore, frequently escalates because parties act on their assumptions, including the assumption that they have communicated clearly and that they have accurately understood the other party's communication. Such assumptions are often mistaken.

Variations in culture, gender, age, class, ethnicity, cognitive capacity, and environment all impact communication. Parties, therefore, often rely on inaccurate or incomplete perceptions and outright stereotypes as the basis of their assessments, judgments, and actions. They may carry, into current communications, the conclusions they have drawn from previous interactions.

Of course, it is possible to improve communication between parties through so-called meta-communication—communicating about communicating—including a reciprocal process of sending and receiving messages about how to communicate, and discussing what is working in an interaction and how to adjust communication to make it work better. But, all too often, the heated atmosphere of conflict is not conducive to such mutual contemplation, no matter how rational. Conflict rarely enhances patience.

Values are beliefs we hold about what is important, what distinguishes right from wrong, and what principles should govern how we lead our lives. They are often deeply-held and reflect our self-identity. Thus, when a conflict is defined or experienced as a dispute over values, it is often interpreted as an attack against our core beliefs, our very self. This makes resolving, let alone transforming, a values-based conflict more difficult, emotionally loaded, and even intractable. To yield in a values-based dispute is perceived as compromising something sacred.

While some conflicts truly involve fundamental differences in values, more often parties *choose* to define the conflict this way. If a party develops a righteous certainty that they hold the moral high ground, their position becomes rigid, and options for resolution melt away. If a true value difference does exist—a less common circumstance than is often thought—parties still have a chance of arriving at an understanding about how to move forward *despite* their value differences. Nevertheless, the core conflict will likely remain unresolved unless circumstances change, values both sides perceive as more important intervene, or one or more parties modify their core values in some way. This may not be necessary, however, if the parties can genuinely agree to disagree, salvage whatever is in their common interest, and move ahead.

Mayer suggests that four contextual factors cut across all sources of conflict:

1. Culture
2. Power
3. Personality
4. Data

To the extent that **culture** is embedded in the parties' communication styles, their history, their ways of dealing with emotions, their values, and the structure within which conflict occurs, it affects the conflict and its prospects for resolution.

Power is the ability to ensure that one's needs are met and the attainment of one's goals is made possible. The dynamics of power can obscure the roots of conflict but can also help parties to understand the nature of the interactions involved in the conflict.

Power is embedded in the structure within which the conflict occurs, and is also a product of **personality**, as this figures in the personal styles and interpersonal interactions of the parties.

Data is embedded in both communication and structure. How data is handled and communicated can ameliorate or exacerbate conflict. Parties can battle for access to data or dispute what data is correct.

As mentioned, human needs are the root causes of conflict. Mayer puts them at the hub of his Wheel of Conflict:

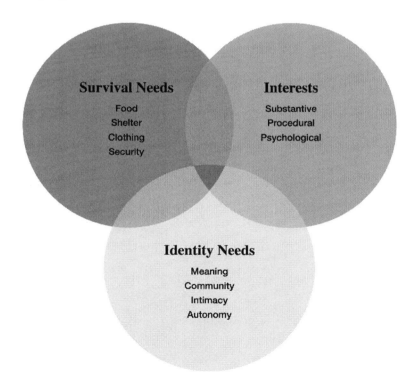

Human Needs in Conflict

Mayer sorts human needs into three overlapping categories—needs relating to survival, identity, and interests—which can assist us in understanding the motivation of parties in conflict.

Interest needs can be short-term, long-term, individual, group, outcome-based, process-based, conscious, and unconscious. In *The Mediation Process: Practical Strategies for Resolving Conflict*, Christopher Moore suggests that interest needs can be substantive (concerned with tangible benefits), procedural (concerned with the process for interacting, communicating, or decision making), and psychological (concerned with how one is treated, respected, or acknowledged).[23]

As for **identity needs**, Mayer points out that these are fundamental to our sense of self, and thus, to our sense of our place in the world. There are four dimensions to our basic identity needs: meaning, community, intimacy, and autonomy.

The need for **meaning** is all about establishing a purpose for our life. Sometimes, pursuing a conflict is a substantial source of meaning, and this may cause a person to hold onto a conflict to avoid the perceived risk of losing personal meaning.

Community refers to that aspect of identity that derives from feeling connected to groups with which we can identify and in which we feel recognized. When people pursue a conflict to solidify a sense of community or to protect their community against the perceived forces of disintegration, they are also struggling to preserve their identity.

Intimacy involves the need to be special, unique, and important to other people. Intimacy needs are mostly met through family and friendship structures. Intimacy implies reciprocity, and, in family disputes, it is often the sudden loss of intimacy or the shattering of the façade of intimacy that causes pain and challenges one's sense of identity. A loss of intimacy may interfere with a party's willingness or ability to accept the outcome of a conflict, especially if the person is not ready to move on from the loss.

The need for **autonomy** is the flipside of both needs for community and intimacy. Autonomy embraces a need for independence, freedom, and individuality. Within families, it is common for tensions to exist between the needs for intimacy and connection versus the countervailing needs for autonomy and independence. These tensions are often manifested as interpersonal conflicts.

When conflicts are identity-based, improving relationships and communication is required to achieve resolution and any possible resolution will be an incremental fix, rather than immediate.

Survival

This brings us back to the most elementary need: survival. Mayer observes that survival needs are concerns for a fundamental sense of safety and security, in addition to a literal requirement for food, shelter, clothing, and the like. Sometimes, the parties to a conflict genuinely feel that their survival is at stake in a conflict—even if this may not be apparent from an external perspective. When any party to a conflict feels their survival is at risk, the others must respond immediately by addressing the perceived or actual threats. No other conflict resolution or conflict management strategy can be effectively employed until this most foundational need is satisfied.

Conflict in Family Businesses

Family business conflicts can partake of any, several, or all of the conflict types that arise in business or in families. Usually, they are multifaceted, with numerous causes that interact in complex ways. This said, relationship conflict, rather than process conflict, predominates in family firms and can often be destructive both to the family business and the family itself.

Before we can dive more deeply into the categories and causes of conflict in the family business and identify means not only of resolving conflict but—when possible—transforming it, we need to identify and describe the dynamics of family business, which is the subject of the next chapter.

CHAPTER 3

THE DYNAMICS OF
FAMILY BUSINESS

I n our highly corporatized world, it is easy to think of the family business as a quaint relic, a business and governance model that is fading if not obsolete. The truth, however, is different from the popular conception. Far from vanishing, family businesses are the predominant form of business enterprise in the world, creating an estimated 70% to 90% of global GDP annually. Recent research suggests that the actual number of family-controlled businesses in the world may constitute 80% of all businesses. In Canada, about half the workforce is employed by family businesses, which are estimated to create 45% to 60% of Canadian GDP, and in the United States, family-owned businesses contribute 57% of GDP, employing 63% of the workforce.[24]

What's in a Name?

Considering the huge role the family business plays in the global, Canadian, and U.S. economies, there is a pronounced lack of consensus as to what, precisely, is meant not just by "family business" but by "family."[25] Instead of venturing into an abstract dictionary definition of either term, we can list characteristics of the family business on which most people would readily agree. Even in the absence of a consensus on definition, most authorities agree that family businesses typically have the following four basic characteristics:

1. Multiple members of the same family are involved as major owners or managers, either contemporaneously or over time.
2. The family controls the business through involvement in ownership and management.
3. The business contributes significantly to the family's wealth, income, and/or identity.
4. The family has intergenerational ("legacy") intent in creating, running, and perpetuating the business.[26]

The fourth characteristic needs some refining. The intergenerational intent of the family business is not necessarily limited to, or strictly defined by, perpetuating any single business or business unit. In the end, however, most families are most interested in creating intergenerational *wealth*. In most cases, this does require a family *business*, which may be a particular store or factory or service provider, but it may also be a portfolio of business interests, including investments. Within the portfolio, it may be common to buy and sell individual businesses.

Let's dig deeper.

In general usage, the term *family business* implies a singular business unit such as a store, an office, or a standalone factory. For many, the phrase "family business" seems almost synonymous with a "mom-and-pop" shop. Yet many family businesses are vast. In Canada, the conflict-ridden Stronach Group definitely falls into this category, but it doesn't even make it into the top 20 Canadian family businesses, the first five of which are:

1. George Weston Ltd. (Weston family)
2. Power Corp. of Canada (Demarais family)
3. Husky Energy (Li family)
4. Empire Co. Ltd. (Sobey family)
5. Bombardier Inc. (Bombardier family)[27]

And if these are not sufficiently impressive, the five biggest family businesses in the world are:

1. Walmart Inc. (Walton family)
2. Volkswagen AG (Porsche and Piech families)
3. Berkshire Hathaway Inc. (Buffett family)
4. Exor NV (Agnelli family)
5. Ford Motor Company (Ford family)[28]

These are all family businesses, but the more appropriately descriptive term for them is "family enterprises." An enterprise may be a very large corporation or, as is fairly common among high-value family businesses, a portfolio of businesses or initiatives in which a family may involve itself. The initiatives in such portfolios often include not only one or more operating business units but, perhaps, portfolios of other assets managed and shared by the family, including financial, real estate, philanthropic, heirloom, and deferred assets. Deferred assets is a special category, highly relevant to family enterprises. These are insurance policies and annuities that that do not come into play until after death. Despite this caveat, they are still very much aspects of the family enterprise.[29]

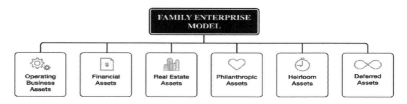

The Family Enterprise Model[30]

You may be surprised to learn that, among family businesses, family enterprises are the worldwide norm, as 89.4% of families control more than a single firm. The mean number of firms controlled by a family is 3.4.[31]

The Complexity of Family Business

Common sense suggests a certain simplicity about a family business. For family business at the "mom-and-pop" end of the spectrum, common sense may be vindicated, but family businesses at the enterprise level, especially those with considerable portfolios, can be elaborate and complex business structures, which is one of the reasons why the litigation in the high-profile Stronach dispute, discussed in Chapter 1, is so tangled.

Complex portfolios and corporate structures are hardly exclusive to family owned and managed enterprises, of course. In the case of the family enterprise, however, an additional layer of complexity comes into play, arising from the effort to balance family demands against the needs of the business while addressing the complex interaction between the two. This, too, is a dramatic aspect of the Stronach dispute. In addition to dealing with the usual business issues—fluctuations in markets, evolving technology, and challenges from competitors—family businesses and enterprises must also navigate the unique psychological dimensions of having family members working together.

Bear in mind that families naturally and inevitably spawn conflicts, and the factor of complexity is almost always a multiplier of conflict. Little wonder, then, that the Stronach saga is unusual only in its scale. If modest family businesses are ripe for conflict, large family enterprises are even more vulnerable.

Each family member in the business has their own characteristics, perspectives, and goals. Working together intensifies the volume and pace of family interactions and can exacerbate such common family problems as sibling rivalry or competition between generations. Couple such unresolved conflicts with diminishing communication and eroding trust, and it is easy to see how conflict can grow out of hand and undermine the operation of the business. Likewise, as the performance of aspects of the family enterprise suffer, family conflict is likely to become increasingly intense, with damage to both the family and the business metastasizing in a vicious cycle.

In the family business, key issues of intrafamilial relations almost automatically translate into problems for the business. Family members with a stake in their family enterprise must take care to:

- Coordinate decision-making across the domains of family, business, and ownership.
- Facilitate long-term family ownership and succession of the business and/or of the family wealth associated with the business.
- Address and resolve issues of nepotism and entitlement.
- Compare the skillsets of family members with those required by the business and manage their involvement accordingly.
- Monitor the performance of family members who have active roles in managing the enterprise.
- Always operate in the best interests of the business and the *whole* family.

Performance of Family Businesses

Time for a deep breath. Yes, the *family* in family business creates certain tripwires and pitfalls. Yet there is ample evidence that the *family* also offers family enterprises unique advantages unavailable to non-family businesses. Research indicates that family firms are often strong financial performers. This is not to minimize the added challenges and the greater complexity that can come with a family business. But while these businesses confront many challenges, they also possess advantages borne out of a unique and dynamic owner-manager-family interaction. Whether measured by bottom-line value creation for shareholders or capacity to create jobs, family companies can outperform their non-family counterparts, and it is not unusual for them to do so.[32]

A 2012 review of 59 empirical studies of the effects of family involvement on the financial performance of firms found that family involvement generally has a positive effect for public family firms and an insignificant or negative effect for private family firms.[33] Another meta-analysis of financial performance found a small positive effect of family involvement on firm performance overall, whether publicly or privately held.[34]

In 1999, Habbershon & Williams developed the concept of "familiness" to describe the unique package of resources that families make available for establishing a strategic advantage in family-run businesses. These "familiness qualities" are particular to family firms and are the result of the unique interaction between the family and the business. The 1999 research suggests that the familiness qualities of family businesses include, but are not limited to:

- long-term strategic focus
- legacy orientation
- family relationships
- operational efficiency

All of these contribute to the strong performance of the firms.[35]

Social Responsibility, Philanthropy, and the Family Business

A lot of big corporations struggle to present themselves as "good corporate citizens"—and many, in all sincerity, doubtless are. But research has shown that, along several dimensions, family firms are often more socially responsible than non-family firms. Indeed, most of the relevant research on this subject shows that family enterprises exhibit higher levels of corporate social responsibility and greater citizenship in the community than non-family firms.[36] Some researchers theorize that this is due to the family's concern about its image and reputation, as well as a desire to protect family assets, which are often bound up with the community.[37]

So-called "legacy families," families characterized by high, very-high, and even ultra-high-net-worth, were the subject of a 2018 Bank of America study conducted in partnership with the Indiana University Lilly Family School of Philanthropy. The study concluded:

> Generosity is the norm among high-net-worth Americans... [T]he overwhelming majority of American high-net-worth households reported making charitable donations. Last year, 90% of this group gave to charity, compared to 56% of the general U.S. population. ... Wealthy donors gave to an average of seven different non-profit organizations in 2017. These donations supported a wide range of charitable causes, with basic needs organizations receiving support from the largest percentage (54%) of high-net-worth households. Additional causes supported by wealthy donors included religion (49%), health care or medical research (36%), combined charities (31%) and youth or family services (29%). Thirty-six percent of high-net-worth households gave to educational causes, including 22% giving to higher education while 24% gave to K-12 education.[38]

Although the 2018 study did not cover Canada, there is no reason to believe that attitudes among high-net-worth families on this side of the border are dramatically different. In addition, another study, which focused exclusively on ultra-high-net-worth individuals (UHNWI), reported that 84% believed that wealthy people have a moral duty to contribute to society.[39] It is well-established that very-high-net-worth and ultra-high-net-worth individuals and families typically devote a substantial fraction of their material wealth to charitable and philanthropic causes. In many cases, wealthy families do not just donate to philanthropic causes and institutions, they create them and play significant roles in their management.

Family enterprises are natural vehicles for philanthropic activity and for the creation and fostering of a philanthropic family identity and legacy. They provide a platform for managing many of the financial aspects of philanthropy, as well as the intangible aspects, including the creation of a social values legacy and the realization of the family's moral and ethical vision. Philanthropy administered through the family business is a gift bestowed on a community, on society, or on humanity itself. At the same time, it is also a gift that the family gives to itself. It is an act of branding of not only the family company or enterprise, but also the family, endowing it with an identity linked to the good causes it funds, perpetuates, champions, and advances. It is, in fact, not uncommon for philanthropy to grow, with a family business, from a sideline to a central focus of the enterprise, its very heart and purpose. A spectacular example is the Tata Group. One of India's largest conglomerates, it was founded as a family company in 1868 by Jamsetji Tata. Today the group comprises 30 companies across the globe and produced US$113 billion in 2019 revenues. Its governance is unique. Tata Sons is the group's principal investment holding company, and 66% of Tata Sons' equity share capital is mandated "to support education, health, livelihood generation, and art and culture."[40] In short, a set of charitable family trusts fund and manage the Tata Group. This family company inverts the customary formula of a standard enterprise operating in a free-market capitalist environment, whereby a portion of revenue is dedicated to philanthropy. In the case of Tata, the capitalist companies of the conglomerate exist primarily for the purpose of funding philanthropy.

Current State of Family Business Research

Interest in family firm research has grown significantly over the last 20 years, establishing an emerging field of study within business research dedicated to how family-owned and family-managed businesses operate and perform. Research directs particular focus to the subsystems that family businesses create. The underlying assumption of this research field is that family firms exhibit unique characteristics that not only distinguish them from non-family firms, but also impact their operation and performance. Agency theory, resource theory, stewardship theory, socio-emotional wealth theory, and institutional theory are some of the central theories making their appearance in the scholarly literature of family businesses.[41]

Among the most intriguing theories to emerge are those guiding the study of the role of socioeconomical wealth ("SEW") in family businesses. These theories hold that, despite the heterogeneity of family firms, a unifying characteristic among them is a focus on non-financial/non-economic value derived from owning and controlling a firm, including "identity, the ability to exercise family influence, and the perpetuation of the family dynasty."[42]

The interdisciplinary research field of family science has been suggested as a resource to help explain how differences among families shape differences among family firms and how family firms, in turn, shape business families. As Peter Jaskiewicz and William Dyer explain, family science is the study of how various elements of familial relationships, family member roles, and family transitions influence outcomes for families.[43] Family business research is still a new and evolving field that is in the process of building legitimacy within management studies.[44]

Another approach to the study of the family business is systems theory. A system is a network of interdependent components that work together for the purpose of achieving the aim of the system.[45] Specifically, five principles of systems theory are relevant to understanding family businesses:

1. The whole is greater than the sum of its parts.
2. Organizations seek homeostasis; they attempt to secure the status quo, keeping things the same or at least stable.
3. Patterns of behaviour are predictable over generations.
4. Every action creates a non-linear reaction, like the ripples created by a stone tossed in a pond.
5. Interfacing life cycles imply constant changes.[46]

In the systems theory approach, the family firm is imaged as comprising three overlapping, interacting, and interdependent subsystems of family, ownership, and management.[47] Each subsystem maintains boundaries that separate it from the other subsystems and the general external environment. The family business operates within these boundaries. This model suggests that a family firm is best understood and studied as a complex and dynamic system in which each of the subsystems has a strong impact on the other subsystems and, accordingly, on the larger system as a whole.

THREE-CIRCLE-MODEL

OF THE FAMILY BUSINESS SYSTEM

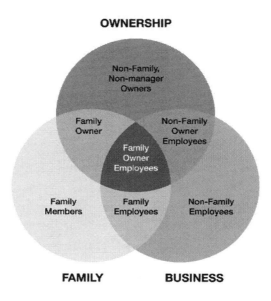

TAGIURI AND DAVIS. 1982

The Three-Circle Model.[48]

If a person has one role in the family or business, they will be in just one subsystem or circle. However, if they have multiple roles, they will be in an overlapping sector, contained within two or three circles at one time.

Within the three-circle model are seven distinct groups with a connection to the family business:

1. Family members not involved in the business, but who are descendants or spouses/partners of owners.
2. Family owners not employed in the business.
3. Non-family owners who do not work in the business.
4. Non-family owners who work in the business.

5. Non-family employees.
6. Family members who work in the business but are not owners.
7. Family owners who work in the business.

Each of the seven interest groups that the model recognizes has its own viewpoints, goals, concerns, and dynamics. The long-term success of a family business system depends on the smooth functioning and mutual support of each of these groups.

Defining Success

For widely held public companies, defining success is often almost ludicrously simple. A *successful* company maximizes the growth in value of the owners' shares—"owners," in this case being defined as institutional and individual investors who have no personal tie to the business. In this view, a successful business is nothing more or less than a fertilizer of financial investment.

By the numbers, however, it is clear that the vast majority of businesses throughout the world are owned, not by external investors, but by people with strong ties to the company. This includes companies owned by founders, by foundations, by partnerships, and by the employees themselves. By the numbers, most of all, this includes family businesses and enterprises.

Few owners in these categories would ever identify the success of their business primarily, let alone exclusively, as maximizing growth in the value of investors' shares. Owners of closely held companies, companies to which they have powerful ties, tend to define success in terms of achieving certain objectives.

Almost always, profit is number one on the list. The reason is simple. Successful companies are profitable. Unprofitable companies are unsuccessful—their lack of success being defined, ultimately, as going out of business.

But profit, while necessary to success, is not sufficient to it, not as far as the vast majority of involved owners are concerned. Typically, additional measures of success include:

- **Creating high-quality products or services**. These are products and services that deliver value for value and perform as promised—or better.

- **Creating loyal customers or clients**. Customer loyalty is strongly tied to the quality of products or services, but it also includes hearing and heeding the voice of one's customers, giving them what they want, creating satisfaction among them, and treating them fairly.

- **Creating positive brand awareness**. Most owners want to become the go-to brand in their market segment. They want consumers to be aware of them and to see value in their company's brand. In part, of course, brand awareness contributes directly to profit, but for involved owners it is also a source of pride, fulfilment, and satisfaction. It is part of the reputation and legacy of the company; for family businesses, this means it is also part of the reputation and legacy of the family.

- **Giving back**. Most owners who are actively involved in their businesses see giving back to their communities as an important dimension of the success of their enterprise. Community involvement ranges from simple charitable donations to full-on programs of philanthropy, up to and including the creation of foundations and the like.

Defining Success for the Family Business

For the owner-managers of closely held non-family businesses, the foregoing list of the dimensions of success is close to being comprehensive and even complete. For the owner-managers of family businesses, however, the listed items are neither more nor less than table stakes. As elements of success, they are necessary but not sufficient.

Successful family businesses place a high premium on the **importance of succession.** In the successful family business, succession planning assumes a key role in the firm's life. In the family business, all dimensions of success simultaneously clamour to be attained. In addition, **competitive business success, family harmony, and ownership returns** are all simultaneously at stake in the firm. This makes skillfully orchestrating a multiyear succession process across generations of owner-managers a high priority.

It should be. It must be.

For, in family-owned companies, business failure is often related to a failure in succession planning. Frequently quoted succession statistics for family businesses are grim. In 1987, Professor John L. Ward, co-founder of the Family Business Consulting Group, conducted a seminal study that found that only 30% of family businesses are successfully transferred to the next generation from the founding owners. Bad as this is, the odds only get worse in the transitions between the second and third generations and the third and fourth generations, when only 13% and 3% of family businesses remain in the founding family.[49]

As the old adage goes, "from shirtsleeves to shirtsleeves in three generations." The phrase encapsulates the theory Ward's statistics seem empirically to support. The first generation of an enterprising family spends its lifetime working hard and living frugally, the second generation enjoys a comfortable lifestyle, eventually entering elite society, and the third generation grows up in luxury, doing little work or none at all while frittering away the family fortune.

The fact is that Ward's 30/13/3 statistic has gone largely unchallenged in mainstream literature and media coverage of family-owned businesses. The implication seems clear: there is something fundamentally wrong with family firms, they are practically destined to fall into the three-generation survival trap.

By no means did Ward misinterpret or distort his findings, but we need to pull back and take a wider-angle view. What we see is that the longevity of family firms is no briefer than that of non-family firms. Survival of both categories of closely held businesses diminish at a high rate after the founders pass on. This does not necessarily disprove or rule out the existence of unique problems in family businesses, but the narrow focus on family business failures over the long term has skewed family business research in ways that have contributed to a negative outlook on family business succession.

Not only has family business research failed to meaningfully compare statistics for family versus non-family firm longevity, but existing family firm survival studies often neglect the portfolio of entrepreneurial activities of business families beyond a core company. The focus is on family business instead of family enterprise. Moreover, most traditional longevity studies fail to acknowledge forms of succession beyond passing on the business within the family. Entrepreneurs who start successful businesses, whether within or outside of a family context, learn the value of running their company as if they intend to sell it. They want their company to be an attractive business proposition. Indeed, many entrepreneurs contemplate an eventual sale as part of a successful business lifecycle. This is also true of family businesses, in which owner-managers regard the sale of one business as a way to harvest value to create new opportunities for the family.[50] Selling a business need not be an act of desperation. On the contrary, it can be a triumph, realizing a substantial return while also ensuring the longevity of the company under new, non-family management.

Wealthy families, so-called legacy families, may do well to think not merely in terms of their family business or family enterprises, but to more broadly plan for the future by thinking in terms of transgenerational wealth.

The concept of family-influenced transgenerational wealth creation reframes succession by turning the focus on developing the family's entrepreneurial tendencies. With transgenerational wealth creation as a goal, the survival of one family firm, a single operating unit or business, is no longer perceived as the only way to pursue and achieve long-term success. In the entrepreneurial model, a number of businesses may be started, acquired, or sold. This cycle inevitably adds to the statistical perception of low succession rates for family firms—but only from the perspective of the individual business unit. When it comes to family enterprise, perhaps it is time to turn to another familiar adage, the admonition to "follow the money." In analyzing the performance of the entrepreneurial family, what target analysts should aim for is not this or that individual business unit but the succession of transgenerational wealth. For, as Zellweger et al. conclude, low succession rates do not necessarily mean that family firms are inept or incapable.[51] If the motive is creating transgenerational wealth through entrepreneurship, the lifespan of the family ownership of any one business unit is an irrelevant or even misleading metric.

Transgenerational wealth creation allows the next generation to use family resources to take risks and build an entrepreneurial orientation. Proactive, entrepreneurial strategies such as diversifying assets through a sale or strategic alliances hardly signify that a particular family business has failed. To grow a family's wealth and pass it on to subsequent generations for their stewardship, the next generation should be given the opportunity to take risks and pursue new directions that are essential for multi-generational growth.

Succession, then, should only be deemed to have failed if the next generation involuntarily loses control of the transitioned assets. In contrast, if a family business is sold and the financial assets are voluntarily redeployed into the financial markets, the sale must be considered an intentional and strategic restructuring of those assets, not a failed succession plan.

Follow the money! And, by the way, if the transitioned financial assets are used for philanthropic purposes, this too must be deemed a voluntary redistribution of those assets—a triumph of a different kind for the family's legacy.

Involuntary losses resulting in succession failure occur only when beneficiaries lose control of their wealth through such causes as "foolish expenditures, bad investments, mismanagement, inattention, incompetence, family feuding, or other causes within their control."[52]

Redefining *Family Wealth* as *Complete Wealth*

There is another dimension to understanding that the successful transfer of intergenerational wealth need not require the transfer of a particular operating business to the next generation. In the context of a legacy family, "wealth" itself should be redefined beyond purely financial assets. There is a family's financial capital, which is a quantitative measure of wealth, but, additionally, a family's *complete* wealth includes such qualitative components as human, intellectual, social, and spiritual capital.[53]

From the perspective of creating and growing the family's complete wealth, accumulating financial capital must be reconceived, not as an end in itself, but as a tool critical to supporting the growth of the family's human, intellectual, social, and spiritual capitals. The key concept of complete wealth is that a family's most important assets are, in fact, its individual members, its human capital.

A family's human capital is simply the members of the family. The human capital value of each member includes their physical and emotional well-being, as well as the individual's ability to find meaningful work and establish a positive sense of identity. In the context of the family, the stewardship of human capital includes effective parenting and grandparenting, communication, consensus building, team building, conflict resolution, leadership training, values, morals and ethics, and goal setting.[54]

Closely tied to the family's human capital, and another dimension of complete wealth, is intellectual capital. This is composed of the knowledge gained through the life experiences of each family member, and what each family member knows. Intellectual capital includes family members' academic successes, career growth, artistic achievements, financial literacy, and the ability to learn and teach what they know.[55]

Social capital, yet another component of complete wealth, refers to family members' relationships with each other and the larger community beyond the family. Social capital also refers to the family's ability to share and sustain an intention that transcends each member's individual interests. This is often manifested in volunteer and philanthropic activities.[56]

Finally, financial capital is the property the family owns. Viewed as an aspect of complete wealth, financial capital encompasses all branches of the family enterprise, including operating business assets, financial assets (cash, public securities, privately held company stock, interests in private partnerships), real estate assets, philanthropic assets, heirloom assets, and deferred assets. Financial capital is the tool that facilitates the cultivation of all other forms of capital that constitute complete wealth.[57]

For the Family Business, Some Games Are Better to Play than Others

Game theory is a branch of mathematics concerned with the analysis of strategies for dealing with competitive situations in which the outcome of a participant's choice of action depends critically on the actions of other participants. Winning conflicts is the goal of game theory—or, at least, minimizing losses in cases where winning is impossible.

Two types of games are recognized in game theory: finite and infinite. Finite games are played to win, and winning marks the end of the game. For example, baseball is a finite game. It has a set of known players, fixed rules, and an agreed-upon objective, which is to win the game. In contrast, the object of infinite games is not to win but to ensure the continuation of play. The rules may change, the boundaries may change, even the participants may change. All of this is fine, provided that the game is never allowed to come to an end.[58]

Family businesses, family enterprise, family entrepreneurship, and creating and growing transgenerational wealth are infinite games. Their objective is not to achieve a game-ending victory, but to perpetuate the game. Now, it is true that finite games are often played within infinite games. For instance, winning a weekly bingo game may be an example of a finite game that contributes to the goal of a larger infinite game, such as maintaining the lifetime friendship of fellow bingo players.

Game play is a metaphor and a logical, conceptual, or mathematical model for complex human engagements whenever they take on both a competitive and cooperative character. Such is the case in family business. Externally, family businesses compete with other firms. Internally, the family business offers various arenas of competition for finite resources, such as income, status, and power. These finite games present opportunities for gain but are also rife with potential for conflict.

How does the family maximize these opportunities while minimizing the risk of conflict?

Family members who compete within the finite game of the business must endeavour to maintain a dual perspective that never lets go of the understanding that they are also playing an infinite game dedicated to perpetuating the family business and/or family wealth to the next generation. If the goal is intergenerational succession of a family business and/or transgenerational succession of wealth, each family member must play in a way that is driven by an overarching mindset of an infinite game. Success is achieved by leading the family business or enterprise so that the business, enterprise, and/or transgenerational wealth survives and grows after the present set of individual players are gone.

CHAPTER 4

CONFLICT IN FAMILY BUSINESS

Researchers widely recognize three general forms of conflict in business, whether family business or non-family business. These are:

1. **Task conflict,** which deals with tensions and disagreements concerning the nature of the tasks that different individuals work on. Such conflicts often manifest as contradicting opinions and views about task goals and technical issues concerning the tasks.

2. **Process conflict,** which deals with disputes over how work should be accomplished. Sometimes, these disagreements focus on the organization of the work and associated plans and timetables.

3. **Relationship conflict,** which deals with interpersonal tensions between individuals caused by their relationship, not by the jobs or tasks they perform or the processes by which these are carried out.[59]

We should note that of the three types, task and process conflicts are usually more readily resolved or transformed than relationship conflicts. This is unfortunate because the source of many, perhaps most, conflicts in family businesses are rooted in relationships. That said, as in any other business, the family business is subject to task and process conflicts as well, which tend to be more emotionally neutral and therefore more readily resolved and even beneficial, opening the way to improving the execution of a task or process. Research confirms that as long as the task of process conflict is present at a moderate level, it prompts debate and discussion that may boost the performance of work and management teams.[60]

The key is moderation. If a task or process conflict escalates, or if these conflicts occur chronically, not only can they degrade the performance of the family business, they can readily mutate into relationship conflict. When this happens, not only will the performance of the business likely suffer, but the conflict may pose a threat to the stability, security, and future of the firm, as well as the family as a unit.[61]

Relationship Conflict

Relationship conflict creates the kind of problems that cause many people to denigrate the very idea of a family business. The naysayers point out that family squabbles—which are relationship conflicts—force family company managers to take their eyes off the ball. Indeed, this can happen. As research shows, relationship conflict tends to shift focus in the organization away from business tasks and business problems to family politics.[62] Leaders of non-family businesses know full well how "office politics" can undermine focus and efficiency. Family politics readily eclipses office politics as a negatively disruptive force. The reason is clear. In a family, relationships are everything, beginning at birth. Family conflicts, therefore, play out for much higher stakes than even the most vicious "office politics." In family business conflicts, the usual business and organizational motives for conflict are still present but are catalyzed and supercharged by "family politics", which have a far longer duration and deeper pedigree rooted in the most basic physiological and psychological needs.

The stakes are high in a family business. There is potentially a lot to lose through conflict, but playing for high stakes also means there is potentially a lot to gain. Recent research recognizes a "familiness advantage" in family businesses, which is, in strategic terms, a force multiplier for productive relationships within a family-run organization.[63] We need to understand that in any business, organization, family, or *family* business, relationship conflicts degrade goodwill, mutual understanding, and camaraderie, leading to reduced satisfaction and diminished regard for other group members. The potential for damage is greater in a family business than in a non-family business. Whatever damage they cause to the family itself, relationship conflicts also hinder the performance of the family firm and especially undermine or even negate the familiness advantage that these companies, under better circumstances, would enjoy.[64]

We will look more deeply into why the familiness advantage is worth fighting for in just a moment, but first we need to clarify the nature of relationship conflicts in family business by categorizing them. These conflicts occur in the form of four general types: justice conflicts, role conflicts, identity conflicts, and succession conflicts.

Justice conflicts revolve around disputes concerning compensation and quality of treatment. Often, one or more parties perceives unfairness in the allocation of resources.

Role conflicts stem from confusion over the roles of the family members working together. When the family also employs non-family members, role disputes can take on an insider/outsider aspect. The same is true when a dispute arises regarding which parties—both within the family and outside of it—are permitted to be or to become owners.

Identity conflicts flow from the need of family members to separate themselves from family expectations and to act with an acceptable degree of independence, autonomy, and individuality. Conflict ensues when there is a failure to balance family expectations and individual identity needs. Such conflicts often manifest themselves as gender conflicts, sibling rivalry, and the multifaceted disputes that arise in relationships between parents and children.

Succession conflicts are encountered in all sorts of businesses but are especially common in family businesses. They are related to issues of ownership and involve which party in the next generation will obtain control over the family firm (power), and the success (or not) of the wealth transfer from one generation to the next.[65]

"Worth Fighting For": A Lesson in Familiness from *Progressive Dairy: Canada*

There is one kind of family business so common that it almost hides in plain sight. It is the family farm. As is the case with the other kinds of family business, many people today look on the family farm as a nostalgic relic of the past. The truth belies the popular conception. In Canada, per the 2011 census, some 150,000 of the nation's roughly 200,000 farms are family-owned. In the U.S., 96% of the nation's 2,204,792 farms are classified as family farms.[66]

In fact, as Jonathan Small, farm management consultant in Red Deer, Alberta, discusses in a 2016 issue of *Progressive Dairy: Canada*, the family farm is a prime example of "the unique bundle of resources a firm enjoys because of the interaction of the family, its individuals and the business with one another." He calls these advantages "worth fighting for."[67] They include:

- "Patient capital"—investment decisions made for the long term.
- A 90% reinvestment rate, which means low debt—a major advantage in farming, often a very high debt enterprise.
- The potential for quicker, more efficient business decision-making, at least if there are no public shareholders.
- A high regard for reputation—pride is taken in the name over the door.
- Opportunity for interfamily alliances.
- Leadership that is generational and creates continuity; management doesn't just have its skin in the game, it's got its DNA there, too.
- Ready access to a potential talent pool.
- Incentive to treat employees "like family" (because they are).
- Employee loyalty decreases costly turnover.
- A customer loyalty advantage, because people like doing business with a family company.
- Commitment and work ethic; overtime goes down easier if the extra hours are yours.
- Natural connection with the community; more supportive of and supported by ones neighbours.
- Potential willingness to try unconventional strategies and tactics; fewer decision makers to persuade.
- Ownership and management are closely aligned.

These qualities do have the makings of a potent advantage, but the issue of succession is, for a family farm, all too often the catalyst for conflict that risks losing it all. Small explains:

> … the prevailing model in farm succession is that farms are either split up among children (losing

many of those ["familiness"] factors), and non-farming children (or just those for whom there is no room) are disenfranchised from the family business in (the sometimes fruitless) pursuit of harmony.

The reasons become apparent when you understand the decision-making styles that tend to be in use in family businesses, especially farms, that are in the hands of controlling owners. Early on in its life, the family business is typically owned and operated by Mom and Dad, and the decision-making model that works is that of an autocrat (aka a benign dictatorship). Mostly (but not always), the parents lead and everyone follows.

When the kids are small, this works just fine. The problem is: Those kids only ever see one example of how it is done from their earliest (and most formative years). No surprise, therefore, that as they become adults and prospective successors on the farm, they know exactly "how it is done," after all they watched Dad and Mom do it that way for 20 or more years.

The problem comes the moment one sibling tries to "autocratically" make a decision affecting another sibling. The cry, "You're not the boss of me" goes up and the wheels, as they say, come off.

The family farm experience teaches that the second generation may model their leadership on the leadership style of the first, which creates conflict because the familial relationship between siblings is very different from that between parents and children. Relationship conflict is created when one sibling attempts to take over the role formerly played by the parents.

Small suggests that things "usually" don't get to this point, however. If the family creates a platform for conflict, it also creates one for avoiding at least some conflicts. Siblings, Small argues, "know from an early age that while they are OK with that [autocratic] style from Mom and Dad because, well, it's Mom and Dad, they will never accept such authority from a sibling (much less a cousin)."

So, either siblings learn to work collaboratively together—they resolve or transform the conflict into an arrangement that permits them to reap the rewards of the familiness advantage—or one sibling sells out to the other. Small points out that sibling partnership farm operations are rare and that, even rarer are "cousin consortiums."

Yet both forms of partnership do exist. What, Small asks, do these rarities have that the others lack? "Interestingly, when you get down to looking at it, they almost always were families where there existed a culture of discussion and consensus-building at a family level. In short, great communication at a family level." The lesson, Small argues, is that "instilling into the next generation that same collaborative/consensus-building style by using it yourselves is one of the best defences against farm breakups. It can be learned later in life, too, but it's easier if that's just the way you grow up."

This applies to succession in all types of family business, not just farms. While family dynamics create possibilities for conflict, they also create unparalleled opportunities for the older generation to model leadership and parenting styles that will help to perpetuate the family enterprise. As Small observes, however, families are in continual transition, as the parental generation ages and the younger generation matures. The actual transition from parent to children usually takes place "in that period when the kids are now in the business, possibly even beginning to own some of it, when they are working with their parents as business partners and no longer as employees." What this means is that *everyone* in the family is obliged to "learn the new style" of leadership, and, faced with this prospect, "many families opt instead for the 'easier' path of splitting the farm or fulfilling the hopes of only a few."

Small finds that many families reject the necessary learning "because those raised in the autocratic style simply cannot accept that it can ever work any other way than a single strong leader." The source of this rigidity? "They have never witnessed anything else."

Small believes that a "family business is a single system," in which "all of the parts are connected to each other." You might think that transitioning the family farm is merely a matter of transferring ownership and responsibilities. He counters that "there are few things more complex than transitioning a family farm because they are more than the sum of their parts." He points out that, in the family business, the "head office [is] the place where the successors themselves (and maybe even a parent) grew up and where all of their childhood memories reside." This creates a dynamic that complicates what would be straightforward decisions in a non-family business. Comparing solving succession in a family business to solving a Rubik's cube, Small points out that "all the parts are connected to each other," so that "you cannot solve it one square or one colour at a time. You have to solve it all at once (holistically)."

Small suggests thinking in terms of the three-circle model, in which ownership, business, and family are connected and overlap, such that decisions made about one circle will have non-linear—that is, disproportionate—effects on the others. Such disproportionate effects too often drive families to give up the fight despite all that the familiness advantage has to offer.

Using the family farm as his example, Small suggests taking the Rubik's cube approach: having a clear goal with a good process in place to reach it. This means starting at the end, by defining everyone's "goals, hopes, dreams or expectations." Instead of getting distracted by details at this point, it is best to develop a broad vision so that everyone—including any outside advisors—is "looking at the same goals (and not assuming what everyone else's are)."

The key first step in understanding and resolving relationship conflict is to establish a common understanding and agree on a common cause. These defined, the next step is to clearly articulate a vision for the future.

Psychology and Family Business

Understanding the psychology of business families and the individuals that make up those families helps to create conceptual frameworks for understanding relationship conflicts. In studying behaviour, two main approaches predominate. The idiographic approach assumes that human behaviour can be meaningfully understood only through uncovering detailed information, whereas the nomothetic approach involves generalizing to gain an appreciation of large-scale patterns.

One of the most influential models of personality, the psychodynamic model, takes an idiographic approach using individual case histories to reach larger conclusions about human nature.[68] Perhaps the most effective way to apply personality theory to family business conflict, however, is to begin from the nomothetic perspective by defining various general themes present in a given dynamic and speculating on how these may be impacting the business family. When you are satisfied that this approach has identified a personality issue that may indeed be driving a conflict, the next step is to shift into the idiographic mode and focus on a specific individual or individuals and their relevant traits.[69]

Both the nomothetic thematic perspective and the idiographic individual perspective can be applied to the framework of the classic three-circle model (business, ownership, and family) to assess the state of a family business at a given point of time. It is a snapshot, and it can be very useful to start a conversation. However, families and family businesses are long-term phenomena, and it is most revealing to convert these snapshots into a video by adopting a developmental perspective. This helps to identify dilemmas and problems that arise because of changes within the business and the family, including the distribution of ownership over time.[70]

Nomothetic Psychodynamic Models

An especially important nomothetic psychodynamic concept to add to the developmental "video" is the family lifecycle, which provides a greater context for the changes that occur over time.[71]

In each of the three subsystems of the three-circle model—ownership, family, and business—there is a separate developmental dimension. A three-dimensional view of the three-circle model takes the developmental dimension into account for each circle. The ownership subsystem goes through a sequence of developmental stages, the family subsystem has its own sequence, as does the business. These developmental progressions influence each other, but they are also independent. Each subsystem changes at its own pace and according to its own sequence. As the family business moves to a new stage in any of the subsystems, it takes on a new shape with new characteristics that impact all three systems.

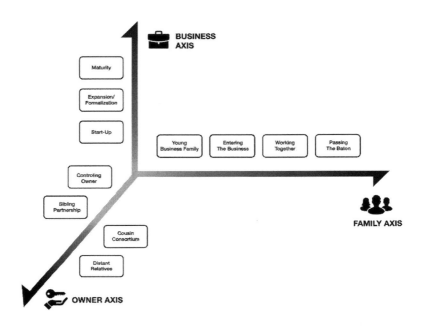

The Three-Dimensional Developmental Model[72]

The three-dimensional model visualizes three axes. The content of the family axis is influenced by the stages of life theories of psychologists Erik Erikson and Daniel Levinson.[73] The owner axis is derived from the work John Ward on how successive stages of family ownership create fundamental differences in every aspect of the family business.[74] The business axis is a synthesis of numerous business lifecycle models. Taken overall, the model provides a framework for understanding family businesses through time in each of the three relevant dimensions, and suggests how understanding both the current stage and the interactions of various stages across the ownership, family, and business subsystems can help provide an accurate analysis of the dynamics of a family business conflict.

Another model, the interfacing life cycles model, builds on the three-dimensional developmental model by adding two more axes, industry and individual.

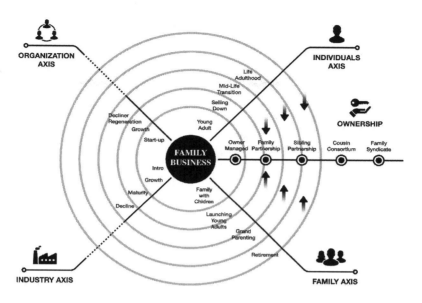

The Interfacing Life Cycles Model.[75]

This model is based on the assumption that the most challenging and even intractable family business issues are not, in fact, business problems the organization faces, but the psychological and emotional issues that compound those problems. By applying this model, we can begin to explain behaviour and enable the family to *prepare* for lifecycle transitions and other issues that may arise in the family business.

Yet another central nomothetic psychodynamic concept is family systems theory, particularly as represented in the circumplex model. Family systems theory describes the family as a system in which members interact through circular communication processes within a hierarchy of established rules and rituals.[76] The circumplex model depicts this family system across three central dimensions: cohesion, flexibility, and communication. The guiding hypothesis of the circumplex model is that balanced family systems tend to be more functional compared to unbalanced systems.[77]

The circumplex model explains family outcomes within a typology of 16 family types based on different levels of cohesion (disengaged versus enmeshed) and flexibility (rigidity versus chaos), which are moderated by the quality of communication. By providing a framework for embracing the range of complexity among families, the circumplex model—and, more generally, systems theory—can assist practitioners in more accurately assessing family relationships and the dynamics underlying conflict in the context of a family business, among other things.[78]

At the core of a family systems model is family cohesion, which is defined as the emotional bonding that family members manifest toward one another. Cohesion is how family systems balance the separateness versus the togetherness of their members. The circumplex model recognizes four levels of cohesion, ranging from disengaged (very low), to separated (low to moderate), to connected (moderate to high), to enmeshed (very high). Central, or balanced, levels of cohesion (separated and connected) make for optimal family functioning. When cohesion levels are very high (enmeshed systems), there is too much consensus within the family and too little independence. In virtually any enterprise, complete consensus is destructive. As the old saying goes, if everybody is thinking alike, nobody is thinking. At the other extreme (disengaged systems), family members go their separate ways, with limited attachment or commitment to their family.[79] This disengaged orientation is also anathema to the effective functioning of a family business.

Family flexibility denotes the amount of change in the family's leadership, role relationships, and relationship rules. Specific measures of family flexibility include leadership (control, discipline) and negotiation styles as well as role relationships and relationship rules. Flexibility is about how systems balance stability versus change. The circumplex model recognizes four levels of flexibility, ranging from rigid (very low), to structured (low to moderate), to flexible (moderate to high), to chaotic (very high). As with cohesion, the theory holds that central or balanced levels of flexibility (structured and flexible) are more conducive to productive family functioning, whereas the extremes—rigid and chaotic—create the most formidable problems for families as they move through their lifecycle.[80]

Communication is critical for facilitating optimal functioning on the dimensions of cohesion and flexibility. Family communication patterns theory provides a framework of four communication patterns along two dimensions, conversation and conformity:

1. The protective pattern (high conformity, low conversation)
2. The pluralistic pattern (low conformity, high conversation)
3. The consensual pattern (high conformity, high conversation)
4. The laissez-faire pattern (low conformity, low conversation)

Research on family businesses has found that high conversation patterns reduce the four types of conflict (task, relational, process, and status), while high conformity patterns increase relational, process and status conflict.[81]

The Big-5 Model: An Idiographic Approach

The models we have discussed so far are nomothetic and focus on psychological and behavioural themes. The Big-5 Model is an idiographic approach, based on individual trait research and its application to behaviour.

Also known as the Five-Factor Model and FFM, the Big-5 Model is a fundamental model of adult personality and represents individual differences in personality by measuring five "macro" traits: openness, conscientiousness, extraversion, agreeableness, and neuroticism.[82] These cover a discrete set of distinctive characteristics:

- **Openness** to experience, which describes the breadth, depth, originality, and complexity of an individual's mental and experimental life.

- **Conscientiousness**, which describes socially prescribed impulse control that facilitates task- and goal-oriented behaviour.

- **Extraversion**, which implies an energetic approach toward the social and material world and includes such traits as sociability, activity, assertiveness, and positive emotionality.

- **Agreeableness**, which contrasts a prosocial and communal orientation toward others with antagonism and includes traits such as altruism, tender-mindedness, trust, and modesty.

- **Neuroticism**, which contrasts emotional stability and even-temperedness with negative emotionality, such as feeling anxious, nervous, sad, and tense.[83]

The effect of these traits on conflict can be complex and context-dependent, particularly when we appreciate the prospect of individual personality differences interacting across the family, business, and ownership subsystems. Certain personality types might be more prone to conflict than others, and different personality types might clash to create conflict. For example, parties who are low on conscientiousness may interact most negatively with those who are high on conscientiousness. Such differences in traits are obvious direct sources of conflict, but personality can also impact conflict more indirectly. For instance, people at loggerheads in a conflict may not simply disagree about a given issue, but may perceive the very nature of the conflict differently. Depending on personality type, one party may see a conflict as task-based whereas another party may see its sources as relationship-based. If we account for the personalities of both people involved, the influence of personality appears even stronger. For instance, differences in levels of extraversion lead to more task-based conflict, whereas differences in conscientiousness are associated with more relationship-based conflict.[84]

The Big-5 Model can help practitioners, as well as family members, predict the likelihood of successfully resolving conflict with one approach versus another. Researchers have, for example, found associations between *collaborative* conflict resolution strategies and higher scores on agreeableness (trust, altruism, compliance) and lower scores on neuroticism (anger, hostility, depression, self-consciousness, and vulnerability). Conversely, *contending* conflict resolution strategies—in which party A persuades party B to concede party A's desired outcome—have been associated with low scores on conscientiousness (competence, duty, self-discipline, and deliberation), low agreeableness (straightforwardness, trust, altruism, compliance, and modesty), low openness (ideas and values), and low extraversion (warmth).[85] Higher scores on all the facets of neuroticism are related to the choice of contending as a conflict resolution strategy. Similarly, neurotic individuals have been found to be more likely to employ attacking strategies or avoid conflict completely.[86]

The Greek philosopher Heraclitus (c. 535 BC–c. 475 B.C.) famously said "Character is destiny." Does this mean, then, that how one fits into the Big-5 Model determines the outcome of a conflict, including the success or failure of a resolution necessary to "save" the family company or even the family itself?

Few psychologists are quite as deterministic as Heraclitus, who is known to history as "the weeping philosopher." Yet most would argue that personality traits, at the very least, put a heavy thumb on the scales of any conflict, decision, or assessment.

Is There an Entrepreneurial Personality?

Character may or may not be "destiny," but personality certainly influences perception, and therefore, plays a role in conflict creation and resolution. So, we may ask, *is a certain type of personality more likely to create a family business than others?* Because family businesses are, by definition, founded by entrepreneurs, we may want to reframe our question this way: *are there common personality characteristics of entrepreneurs that can inform those (practitioners or family members) who are working to resolve or transform a family business conflict?* Is there an entrepreneurial personality?

Many studies have, in fact, been made to assess whether there are common personality characteristics of entrepreneurs. The most recent evidence suggests that the typical personality traits that manifest in entrepreneurs vary depending on the type of entrepreneurial activity in question. For instance, entrepreneurs who found technology start-ups don't necessarily share a unique "entrepreneurial personality" with those who start mom-and-pop businesses.[87] Put simply, not every founder of a family business will exhibit the personality traits of a Steve Jobs or an Elon Musk.

Within the family business realm, thousands of founders seek growth-oriented family businesses and many more seek to build a business for their families as self-employed proprietors. Neither of these descriptors strike one as adequate characterizations of a Jobs or a Musk. Nevertheless, a recent meta-analysis of 23 studies conducted from 1970 to 2002 in a variety of countries found that "entrepreneurs" in every type of business tend to be more open to experience, more conscientious, less agreeable, and less neurotic than "managers." Only in the area of extraversion were entrepreneurs and managers found to be "similar."[88]

Other studies have assessed whether entrepreneurs differ from the general population in such qualities as self-efficacy, innovativeness, internal versus external locus of control (or LOC), risk attitudes, and need for achievement. Recent studies indicate that an internal LOC (a belief that one controls one's own life) and a need for achievement are important predictors of entry into entrepreneurship. Risk-taking also correlates with business founding but not necessarily with performance or exit. Finally, there seems to be a link between entrepreneurial self-sufficiency and business founding, as well as with specific related functions such as business planning skills.[89]

The personality traits associated with entrepreneurs, most people would agree, are positive, affirmative, and generally desirable traits. But is there a downside to what we might call the entrepreneurial personality?

It is true that entrepreneurs who found family firms can be creators of enormous wealth for their family members, employees, and society itself. Entire industries and game-changing innovations have been driven by entrepreneurs, including founders of family firms. What they create for their families may have lasting economic and lifestyle impacts on society. To start a business from scratch, let alone to disrupt an entire industry, requires a high appetite for risk and enormous initiative, drive, and fortitude in the face of many and daunting obstacles.

What could possibly be wrong with any of this?

The positive personality traits of family firm entrepreneurial founders do have a dark side. Specifically, such positive attributes as high energy, self-confidence, need for achievement, and self-sufficiency can devolve over time into over-confidence, aggressiveness, narcissism, ruthlessness, and irresponsibility.[90] Practitioners who counsel business families frequently encounter the theme of the aggressive, impatient, demanding, authoritarian, neglectful parent who is also the business founder/patriarch.[91] The personal qualities that drive initial success are also the personal qualities that contribute most to creating the conflict.

Organizational Conflict

Because family conflict is present in most instances of conflict among business families, we can conclude that relationship conflict is at the root of conflict in family businesses. Even such non-relationship conflict as that associated with tasks and process readily mutates into relationship conflict in the context of family businesses. That said, both families and family businesses are organizations, and, accordingly, family businesses are hardly immune to the kind of organizational conflict that also afflicts non-family enterprises.

Gary Johns of Concordia University and Alan M. Saks of the University of Toronto inventory the following major causes of organizational conflict, which are the causes most commonly studied and researched:[92]

- **Group Identification and Intergroup Bias:** Many types of groups are found in any given organization. Some are based on race, gender, or age; others on job functions or job level. In part, group identification and bias are self-imposed, but the differences—and potential sources of conflict—between groups are emphasized by differences, actual or perceived, in power and opportunity associated with a given group.

   People tend to have a positive view of their own group, which may lead to an invidiously negative view of other groups. Generally, the more the members of one group perceive other groups as essentially different from them, the more negative their perception of the other group or groups. Intergroup bias is strongly related to self-esteem, such that a member of one group tends to see that group as more successful than any other.

   Families often develop cliques, and the organization of a family business may foster such developments. Family businesses need to recognize the importance of managing relationships between groups or teams within the family business. Moreover, family business leadership should find ways of attenuating the perceived differences between individuals so that the motive for proliferating cliques or groups is reduced.

- **Interdependence:** In any group, interdependence can be a source of perceived strength or a major cause of conflict. A common example of such interdependence is illustrated in sales and production groups, for instance. The sales team has no choice but to depend on the production team to supply it with product, whereas, for its part, production requires sales to provide demand by making sales and by reporting sales in a timely manner, so that production can meet demand. The two functions are effectively joined at the hip. If sales fail, production suffers—and vice versa. The potential for conflict here is entirely due to dependence. If the two functions, sales and production, were independent of one another, there would be no conflict between them.

  In a family business, there is added incentive for interdependent functional units *not* to fail one another. Yet this also amps up the kind of emotional pressure that creates or exacerbates conflict. Interdependence can increase organizational cohesion or tear an organization apart. The key is for everyone involved to embrace interdependence and let it drive understanding of the necessity for efficient interaction and coordination. When interdependence works well, it creates productive and rewarding collaboration through mutual assistance. When one function fails another or is perceived to abuse its power however, antagonism and friction develop, leading to destructive conflict.

- **Difference in power:** While interdependence can create conflict, it can also create effective collaboration. In relationships that are driven not by interdependence but by a one-way dependence, the probability of conflict significantly increases. In such unequal power relationships, conflict frequently occurs when one individual or group must accomplish a goal, but the individual or group upon which it depends is not aligned on the same goal. This frustration of achievement triggered by a one-way power relationship readily explodes into antagonism. Production units are sometimes frustrated in this way by quality control units. If production cannot get the approval of quality control, a conflict may occur. In the family business, the second generation may find itself hobbled by a "patriarch," who refuses to approve a certain initiative. In such a case the difference in power is both organizational and familial, and thus creates a conflict with multiple dimensions.

- **Difference in status:** Even in modern business organizations that take pride in flat, as opposed to hierarchical, management structures, differences in status exist. The structural imperative is for individuals of lower status to accept and act upon orders from those with higher status. Sometimes, individuals with lower status may give orders to those with higher status. Insofar as this runs counter to the structure of organization, conflict may develop. In the family business, the hierarchical structure of the organization may be reinforced by the family hierarchy. When a daughter gives an order to the father, conflict may develop.

- **Difference in culture:** Families are not immune to cultural differences and resulting conflicts. These are often intergenerational. The older generation may have a very different attitude to customer relations than the younger, and this difference may create antagonism and conflict. Another source is cultural difference between different business functions. Sales culture may conflict with the culture of those who manage credit.

- **Ambiguity:** Lack of clarity—or ambiguity—is a virtually universal source of conflict. Absence of clear decisions, policies, and communication leads to assumptions and guesswork replacing information concerning goals, plans, and procedures. Typically, this type of conflict develops between managers and employees.

- **Scarce resources:** Scarcity of resources is a cause of conflict in societies, families, businesses, and family businesses. When resources are scarce, internal competition develops in the organization, which often leads to open conflict. In the family business, such competition can cross over into patterns of familial competition, such as sibling rivalry and power struggles between the generations.

Identifying the sources of conflict and defining the interfaces between family conflict and business conflict are the first critical steps toward resolving conflict and even preventing or averting it. This is the subject of the next chapter. The final chapter, Chapter 6, takes the engagement of conflict in the family business to the next level, moving it from both resolution and prevention to transformation, the productive use of conflict to improve the performance of the family business and the family itself.

CHAPTER 5

PREVENTION AND RESOLUTION

On the face of it, preventing conflict in a family business seems like a self-evidently desirable goal, but John Lederach warns us in his *Little Book of Conflict Transformation* that preventing conflict or even "resolving" conflict carries with it "a danger of co-optation, an attempt to get rid of conflict when people [are] raising important and legitimate issues."[93] From the outset, then, it is best to recognize that while conflict poses a significant threat to family businesses and the family itself, the threat may be even graver if prevention and resolution are used to evade and avoid dealing with the critical issues at the heart of a looming or ongoing dispute. Ignoring, denying, or even treating a symptom does not address the underlying disorder. Moreover, as conflict experts like Lederach argue, whatever threat of harm a conflict may present, it is often also an opportunity for more than resolution. It may be a chance for positive transformation.

This chapter is about building on the understanding of conflict in family business demonstrated in Chapter 4 to address aspects of organization and relationship that can be improved or corrected before they create conflicts that are better avoided. The chapter is also about engaging conflict in ways that do not deny, evade, or suppress legitimate issues, but prevent the resulting conflict from exploding into something highly and perhaps irreversibly destructive. Most emphatically, this chapter is not about creating harmony or homogeneity in lockstep and at any cost. For one thing, conflict is inevitable and for another, it is not all bad. We upright bipeds walk, making forward progress by continually destabilizing and restabilizing ourselves, falling forward and arresting our fall just in time to propel ourselves into the next progressive fall that propels us to our goal. So it is with progress in any meaningful endeavour. We disagree, we address the sources of conflict, we allow this temporary instability to advance the enterprise.

This chapter is intended to assist advisors, practitioners, and family members themselves to prevent or remediate conditions that provoke unnecessary and unproductive conflict and to ensure that when conflict does arise it is limited in its destructive effect and addressed in productive ways that advance the business and the family.

Good Governance

In nations, good government is essential to preventing conflict from becoming destructive. In family businesses, good governance serves the same purpose.

Governance is an organizational structure designed to aid groups in making decisions. It is a system that establishes the structures, processes, plans, statements, policies, rules, and agreements intended to be used to pursue the objectives of the organization.[94] The guiding principle behind good governance is twofold, each element of governance should contribute to both efficiency and fairness. That is, each should facilitate rather than impede decision making, and each should ensure that every stakeholder is heard, recognized, respected, and treated justly.

Common sense suggests that governance in a *family* business should be easier than in a publicly owned enterprise. As is so often the case, however, common sense is mistaken. Family business governance is, if anything, more complicated than governance in non-family owned companies. As mentioned in Chapter 4, the *family* in family business can (and, statistically, does) provide a "familiness" advantage that confers a performance edge on family businesses. Yet the family also adds a layer of complexity to the business, which increases the chance of conflict. For this reason, governance of the family business must be seamlessly integrated with governance of the family itself. The essentials of family business governance, therefore, include regular family meetings and a family charter or constitution.

Regular Family Meetings

By implementing meetings at regularly established intervals in which family members can communicate with each other in a structured environment, the family creates a system that facilitates open communication and prevents or corrects miscommunication. This will itself prevent many a preventable and unnecessary conflict. Equally important, regular meetings allow developing conflicts to surface and the issues to be discussed and addressed before a potentially destructive conflict spirals up the conflict ladder.

Families are as varied as their members, which means that when it comes to the appropriate format for the family meeting, one size does not fit all. Working collaboratively, perhaps even with an advisor or within the context of a family office, the family itself should design a form of meeting that works for them and incorporates their preferred communication style. Today's digital technologies enable geographically far-flung families to meet more frequently and with less investment of money and time, via such software as Zoom, Microsoft Teams, Google Hangouts, and so on, but, for business families, at least some of the regular meetings should be in-person and include such features as facilitated family councils and family retreats.

It is all too easy to forget that family life includes as much joy as its members want to bring to it. Family business meetings can be combined with family pleasures, including dinners, vacations, and reunions.

Family meetings can be coordinated through a regularly issued family newsletter—or blog or forum—which can be distributed by mail or, far more conveniently, posted online. This is an effective way to keep geographically dispersed family members connected through personal updates, photos, and videos, as well as up to date on business or financial information.

Fake fun is no fun, and if the family is in an elevated state of conflict, family meetings should be carefully and deliberately planned in advance and, preferably, facilitated by a trained third party.[95]

The Family Constitution or Charter

Some call it a constitution, charter, protocol, creed, or just plain family agreement. The name is not important. What matters is that it is a central document, on which all family members agree, that sets out the family's values, vision, and commitment in relation to the family business. It is also the record of the agreement the family has reached on such key business issues as who can own shares in, or work for, the family business. Family charters are not typically binding legal documents—though they may certainly be brought into evidence in legal disputes— rather, they are memoranda of agreements in principle and, equally important, expressions of the aspirations of the business-owning family.

In the family constitution, members define and articulate their shared goals and the shared guiding values and principles that will help them to achieve those goals. The constitution is a foundational document that aids in the maintenance of business sustainability and can be useful in preventing conflict through misunderstanding or misremembering. A constitution can reveal to the family the valuable fact that it works and dwells within a mental and emotional region comprised more of agreement than of conflict.

Consider the family constitution as the family's values and vision made public. In this sense, it is much like the family business itself, which can likewise be viewed as the external manifestation of a family's value system.

For a family, values are effectively shared rules for living. Upon these, a family vision and business mission are raised, and they inform the family's business-related decision making. When the family and its business confront challenging times, vision and values go a long way toward holding things together. Without clarity of shared values and vision, the odds of the eruption of destructive conflict increase.[96] It is hard to remember who you are and what you stand for when you have no record of who you are and what you stand for.

Using a constitutional document to codify the family's vision and values becomes increasingly important with the passage of time. As families expand and scatter geographically and culturally, as one generation gives way to the next, it is important to review, revive, and, as necessary, revise the shared values that bind family members to one another and to the business.

In running its business, the family typically communicates its vision and values to the board, which sets strategies and implements actions accordingly. With shared vision and common values set forth in a constitution to inspire and inform business performance, a virtuous circle can be created. When family members see their values strengthening their business, their pride in those values and the family that lives them is reinforced and amplified. Research shows that a strong family constitution, a protocol aimed at improving the members' coexistence and cohesion as a family, is positively related to business performance.[97]

Governance Structures for the Family Business

Governance in a family enterprise can refer to the overall conduct of the family business system or to any of the more specific types of governance found in each of the three subsystems in a family business system.[98]

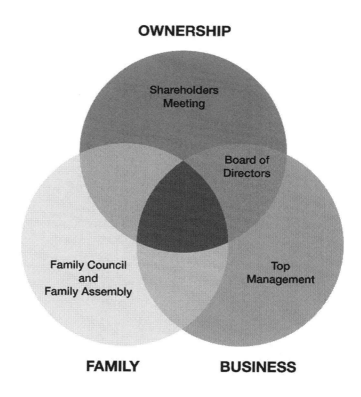

The Basic Governance Structures
of the Family Business System Model[99]

The evolution of many family businesses is a movement away from unilateral decision making in the owner-founder stage and toward more complex decision making in (for example) the sibling partnership and then the cousin consortium stages. In such an evolution, increased and more formalized governance becomes important to ensure that the right people are given the right information to make the right decisions. The three systems of governance do not necessarily need to be in place all at once, nor must they necessarily operate simultaneously in one family enterprise. The governance structure a family firm needs at any one point depends on the developmental life stage of the business. Needs at inception (the owner-founder stage) are different from those during, say, a sibling partnership (growth stage), and both are different from what is required in a cousin consortium (the harvest stage).[100]

Although one type of governance structure does not fit all family enterprise systems, most can be governed by some version of the following structures.

Family Circle Governance

The governance needs of family businesses depend on quantitative factors—such as family size, business complexity, and the balance between insiders and outsiders—and qualitative factors, such as the degree of cohesion and quality of communication among family members. Smaller, more cohesive families may start their governance simply by having frequent family meetings, whereas families of greater size and geographical footprint, or those involving greater tensions likely require a more formalized approach from the get-go, including the guided negotiation of family charters and shareholder's agreements.

Family circle governance may operate through one or both of the following structures:

- **Family Assembly:** Also called family meetings, family forums, family briefings, family gatherings, family retreats, or family conventions, a family assembly is a meeting of the wider business family. Attendance is usually open to all adult family members, whether they actively work in the business or just hold shares in it.

  As noted, family meetings are essential in any family enterprise and are perhaps the single most effective forum for averting the most common causes of conflict. As family members participate in creating their shared future through family meetings, these events become the occasions by which trust and communication are strengthened. They also serve to prepare the rising generation for their future roles and responsibilities and to reinforce shared values and develop a shared vision.

- **Family Council:** A family council is an advisory and consultative body representing the business-owning family. Its key role is to facilitate communication between the family members and the board of directors. Usually, the family council also organizes the meetings of the Family Assembly.

Ownership Circle Governance

The ownership subsystem comprises the actual equity owners of the family enterprise. Business ownership may be visualized as a package of rights and responsibilities attached to share or asset ownership. Arguably, the chief responsibility of business owners is to provide capital to the firm. In most jurisdictions, in exchange for capital, shareholders are given rights, such as the right to attend and vote at shareholder meetings, to receive dividends, and to elect the board of directors, which has the primary responsibility of managing the business.

Ownership in family businesses tends to progress through a sequence of continuity:

1. Owner-managed businesses in which ownership of the company is in the hands of just one person.
2. Sibling partnerships where ownership has been divided more or less equally among a group of siblings, some or all of whom work in the business.
3. Cousin companies (third-generation firms and older) in which ownership has been spread across a group of shareholders, a significant proportion of whom take no part in the day-to-day management of the business.[101]

Added to the incremental stages of ownership of a family enterprise are the six types of owners:

1. An operating owner with direct responsibility for running the business.
2. A governing owner, who is a full-time overseer but not involved in the family business, such as a chairman of the board of directors.
3. An involved owner, who is not employed in the business but takes a genuine interest in the company, offering support to management as appropriate.
4. A passive owner, who collects dividends but abdicates responsibility for the business to others and makes no conscious decision to stay an owner.
5. An investor-owner, who is similar to a passive owner; except, if they are dissatisfied with their returns, they may make a deliberate decision to keep or sell ownership.
6. A proud owner, who is not engaged in the business or especially knowledgeable about it, but nonetheless is proud to be an owner.[102]

In addition to the type of owners noted above, owners can be differentiated along a growth versus harvest continuum of motivation. A **harvest strategy** is associated with optimizing returns today in terms of resisting investment in the business, eschewing risk and market development, and extracting maximum dividends.[103] In contrast, a **growth strategy** is associated with optimizing revenue and share appreciation in the future in terms of maximizing investment in products, capabilities, and markets of the business, albeit with greater risk.[104] Research has found that owner-founders pursue a growth orientation while subsequent generations of owners trend toward greater harvest orientation as ownership disburses.[105]

- **Shareholders Assembly/Owners Council:** The governance structure for the ownership subsystem is an owners council or shareholders assembly, which consists of representatives elected by the group of owners. This council is the foundation of the governance system for the business. The ownership council has the authority to choose members of a board of directors or a board of advisors, as well as the chairperson of either of these boards. If the business is still in its inception, or owner-founder stage, an ownership council may even include family members who are not technically "owners" at all. This allows decision-making to be distributed beyond the single owner-founder.

  The ownership council addresses anything related to ownership of the company including decisions on behalf of all shareholders, liquidity issues, generational, continuity and transition issues, and how to execute the family's long-term vision. Shareholders meetings including all shareholders are held as a method of communication between the shareholders council and the larger ownership group.

Business Circle Governance

There is a clear link between best-practice business governance and conflict prevention. Business governance often starts with an informal board of advisors before it transitions to a formal board of directors.

- **Board of Advisors:** Having a board of directors is a legal requirement of incorporated companies in most jurisdictions and is the primary governance structure for any incorporated business, family-owned or not. During the early stages of a family business, the board mainly functions as a statutorily required legal entity and is, in fact, often a rubber stamp for the owner-operator. Over time, it often transitions into an advisory board, comprised of trusted employees, professional advisors (such as the company lawyer and accountant), and friends. The function of an advisory board is to provide a sounding board for the founder's ideas and concerns over the direction of the business. Usually, an advisory board is an interim solution between a fully family-run board of directors and a board with one or more formally appointed non-executive outside directors. An advisory board allows for a transition in the formality of the way a family business operates and the degree of accountability and challenge an owner-founder faces as leader.

- **Board of Directors:** As the business grows and ownership and management roles are separated, the board of advisors often becomes more formal and professional in its role and functions as more than a legally required rubber stamp. It now provides feedback, confirming management's actions, planning continuity, and assessing performance. An effective board of directors facilitates conflict prevention in two fundamental ways. It holds management accountable for early planning, and it demonstrates to the next generation that the family is committed to both increasing professionalism in ownership and management, and to accepting new ideas.

Legal Planning

In addition to good governance, legal planning—proactive and preventative—may allow the business to avoid a world of costly and protracted familial and financial disputes. Fundamental planning tools include those that provide for retirement and death, such as shareholders' (or partnership or other co-ownership) agreements, trusts, outright gifts, as well as marriage agreements and wills. Additional planning tools provide for instances of incapacity. These include trusts, powers of attorney, and delegation of corporation authority.

Here are the main planning tools a family business needs to proactively pre-empt much legally based conflict:

- **Shareholders' Agreements:** A comprehensive shareholders' agreement is a key tool for preventing conflict or effectively managing what conflict may come, especially concerning issues of succession. The agreement may also serve as a tool to reinforce family governance strategies put in place to facilitate intergenerational participation in the business. By providing safeguards against the potential risks inherent in permitting the next generation to acquire ownership in a business, the agreement can facilitate broader ownership of the family business.

  In essence, a shareholders' agreement sets out the rules for co-ownership of any family enterprise. The agreement governing a family business that aspires to extend to multiple generations must address the various events that typically occur in the life of a family: marriage, illness, disability or incapacity, divorce, difficulty with creditors, retirement from the family business, and family disputes. Key to such an agreement is the flexibility to adapt to changes in the circumstances of both the family and the family business.

Many family-owned businesses have no shareholders' agreement in place, particularly in the early years. During this phase, owners rarely believe that such an agreement is necessary because succession is not yet a priority or because they believe that family members will reach agreement when necessary. Nevertheless, the best time to implement a shareholders' agreement is while the founder-owner is still alive, capable, and in control of the business. Unfortunately, too many business owners appreciate the need for a shareholders' agreement only when it is suddenly needed because a dispute has arisen—which (it becomes apparent) such an agreement could have resolved or avoided.

- **Trusts:** Creating a trust has many benefits, including:

  1. Centralized asset ownership and management of assets
  2. Flexibility in determining the method of future wealth distributions
  3. Enhanced asset protection for beneficiaries from third-party claims, including potential creditor and other actions
  4. Increased confidentiality
  5. Potential avoidance of probate procedure and consequent probate fees

A key feature of a trust is the separation of ownership and control of an asset from the beneficiary of that asset. This makes the trust useful in the preservation of wealth and the succession of the family business. The founder of the family business is able to direct which elements of the business are to be transitioned to the next generation or other parties, transfer those elements into a trust, retain control of them by acting as trustee, and, as and when the founder considers appropriate, make distributions out of the trust. In this manner, the founder can affect the transition of ownership gradually, retaining the flexibility to respond to changing circumstances.

There are many complexities inherent in trust drafting and interpreting the applicable tax rules. A professional tax planner is required.

- **Marriage Agreements:** When a marriage or marriage-like relationship breaks down, a division of spouses' property is made. The impact on a family business can be significant and may even challenge or end its viability. Family members often wish to keep the business in the family, which means out of the hands of an estranged spouse. A well-drafted marriage agreement can reduce the risk of an estranged spouse acquiring an interest in the business, and therefore is an important part of conflict mitigation for the family enterprise.

    In the context of the family enterprise, the main objective of a marriage agreement is to ensure that the business interests or other assets, whether held directly or indirectly (through a trust, of which the family member spouse is a beneficiary), remain, upon martial dissolution, the property of the family member spouse.

    If a marriage agreement is to achieve the desired result, it is critical that each spouse fully and mutually disclose their individual assets as a pre-condition of signing the agreement. Transparent and full disclosure will face impediments if a founder does not wish to disclose valuations to her child or grandchild, if the interest is in a discretionary trust and is therefore difficult to quantify, and/or if the expense of formally valuing the business interest would be prohibitive.

Even with full and accurate financial disclosure, a well-drafted agreement, and both parties obtaining independent legal advice, there can be no guarantee that the agreement will escape judicial intervention upon marital breakdown. That said, some agreement is certainly better than none, and can serve as a valuable communication tool for family members and their spouses on the nature of family enterprise assets, their value, and family expectations in terms of succession planning.

- **Other Tools (Including Wills):** Some additional pre-emptive, preventative legal planning strategies to consider include:

  1. Rearranging property ownership
  2. Joint tenancy ownership
  3. Life insurance with specific beneficiary designations, or life insurance trusts
  4. Annuities
  5. Registered Retirement Savings Plans (RRSPs) and RIFs
  6. A will

A will is an essential part of a plan to distribute an estate on death, but it is only one part. Arranging property interests in different ways during one's lifetime can accomplish some or all of the intended distribution. A will, however, must be drafted to accommodate the overall estate plan.

Even if a complex estate plan has been put into place with trusts and other structures, there are almost always some assets that have not been dealt with and which must be addressed in the will. In addition, a will appoints an executor, who has legal authority to administer an estate, including defending or pursuing any legal claims against the estate. Common planning for families who own private businesses is to enter into multiple wills, with corporate assets governed by a second, non-probated will. It is essential that such planning be carefully considered in terms of drafting and income tax considerations to prevent unforeseen conflicts later. No matter how simple or complex an estate plan is, a will is essential for all family business planning.

- **Incapacity Planning and Power of Attorney:** Failing to plan for incapacity can result in significant damage to the assets and the operational health of a business if incapacity triggers conflict between family members. If, in the absence of the required documents, there is a dispute about who can sign for a founder or a president, it may become necessary to appoint a committee or adult guardian for that family member. This is not only time-consuming, but could degrade the viability and goodwill of the business.

  Execution of an enduring (called "durable" in the U.S.) power of attorney in advance of any incapacity confers authority to carry on the incapacitated family member's legal and financial affairs. Execution of multiple powers of attorney, including one that provides limited powers to carry on the business, should be considered. This way, a separate attorney can be appointed to manage each of the business and personal assets and thus permit the smooth continuity of a business in the event of the unexpected incapacity of a key person or a family conflict.

Family Office for Integrated Wealth

A family office is a fast-growing solution that allows the higher-net-worth family to manage and transfer wealth in a cohesive and planned manner. Consolidating asset management, governance, family communication, education, and philanthropy into one entity is a sophisticated strategy for pre-empting conflict and promoting the continuity of transgenerational wealth.

The family office is a means by which a family coordinates its financial affairs. The decision to create a family office is usually motivated either by a requirement for coordination of the liquid portion of wealth or by a significant increase in family liquidity and the desire to retain some degree of control over the management of the proceeds of that occurrence. A family office enables the family to maintain control over how they preserve and grow their wealth and, at the same time, serves as a single focal point of contact for the family and their numerous advisors.

In essence, the family office is designed to meet the unique needs of the family that it serves, which means that every family office is different. As is commonly said, "If you've seen one family office, you've seen one family office."

Generally, a family office is a separate entity committed to sustaining and building the long-term wealth of a family. It does this by drawing on a collection of advisors and a professional team to manage, sustain, and grow family assets while preparing future generations to be thoughtful and productive stewards of those assets. Family offices can provide a wide range of services based on a family's needs, including, but not limited to, wealth management, estate and legacy planning, family communication, education and governance, and tax compliance and filing.

The family office acts as a single conglomerate for the many systems required to manage family wealth. It can also serve a number of roles on behalf of the family that go beyond the basics of wealth management. Typically, it acts as the keeper and executor, the guardian and confidant, and the brain trust for the family.[106]

As the keeper and executor, the family office executes and archives various transactions and legal documents related to family wealth. One of the key benefits of a family office is that it allows families to manage their wealth as they would a unique business, such that the family office, rather than an individual family member, manages tasks and transactions relating to family wealth.

The family office also provides a single, secure location to collect, amass, and archive all relevant family documents. These may include any tax, compliance, legal, business planning, investment planning, and estate planning documentation.

Next, as the guardian and confidant, the family office serves to protect the family from risk and to work in the best interests of the *whole* family. As a family amasses wealth, it also amasses risk, especially as systems become increasingly complex. A family office integrates wealth and family management systems, allowing for increased communication between systems and more complex risk assessment and conflict prevention and management.

First and foremost, the family office is a protector and steward of the family wealth. This involves, in part, proper identification and mitigation of risks by creating an environment in which advisors in various fields of family wealth management are enabled to share knowledge in service to the family.

Research in the field of family business advising confirms that communication and knowledge-sharing among advisors across multiple disciplines leads to more effective advising in all disciplines and a reduction in conflicts.[107] Many issues that arise in family business relate to more than one component system, which requires the attention of multiple advisors. Communication among advisors, facilitated by the family office, is key to the identification, analysis, and solution of problems and conflicts.

Finally, as the family's brain trust, the family office serves as a repository of family knowledge and development. As noted, family wealth is not measured only in liquid assets but also by the experience and knowledge each family member possesses. The family office provides a structured organization for compiling this knowledge and using it to further family and individual successes.

The brain trust's knowledge can be exchanged through family meetings, fostered through family education, and passed on by knowledgeable family members and trusted advisors. Having access to the wide network of family knowledge benefits each individual member of the family in achieving their personal goals and strengthens family bonds and communication by giving voice and value to the knowledge and experience of each family member.

- **Family Office Services:** Families decide what specific services they want from their family office. Generally, these services are expressly designed to address the many needs of transgenerational wealth. There is a need to preserve and build family wealth, and an equally pressing need to prepare the family to receive and become responsible stewards of this wealth.

Family office services most commonly include:

- Family meeting coordination
- Development and maintenance of governance structures
- Family education
- Conflict prevention and conflict management
- Tax, estate and financial planning
- Wealth transfer planning
- Asset protection and other risk management
- Investment consulting, monitoring, and performance measurement
- Philanthropic planning and foundation management
- Financial recordkeeping, compliance, and consolidated reporting.

- **Family Office Structures:** The most common family office models are the single-family office (SFO), the multi-family office (MFO), the private asset manager, and the customized family office. Each offers different strengths and each appeals to different family needs, desires, and capacity to finance these. Savvy families and their advisors see a common strength of the family office as an invaluable conflict prevention and conflict mitigation tool, especially for business families that want to consolidate their business affairs (and/or wealth) in a centralized and formal manner.

Conflict Management in a Family Business

Despite taking steps to pre-empt conflict, conflict *will* happen in the family business. Based on the nature of the conflict, its intensity, and care for other parties, family members can choose from five styles of conflict management:

1. Collaborative
2. Competitive
3. Avoidance
4. Accommodative
5. Compromising[108]

How a conflict is managed is a function of how assertive a party is in satisfying their own group or self-concern versus how cooperative they are in satisfying those of the other party:[109]

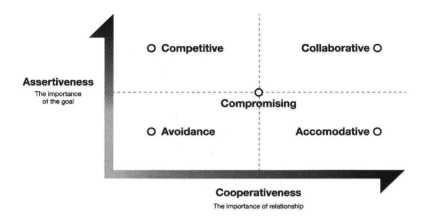

Approaches to Managing Organizational Conflict Model[110]

The **avoidance** style of conflict management has both the lowest cooperation with other parties and lowest assertiveness of a party's own interests. This style is not to be confused with taking proactive steps to *prevent* conflict. Rather, it is a style born of a desire to hide from a situation or to take steps to avoid immediate stress. It rarely addresses underlying conflict sources. It does have an advantage in cooling down a conflict, even when there are no clear solutions. Indeed, avoidance, which is based on distancing from problems, can be effective for small problems and for difficult and escalating problems that have no clear or immediate solution.

The **accommodative** style is seen whenever there is total cooperation with the other party while not asserting one's own concerns. This is not necessarily a sign of weakness. In some situations, it may well be the best and most suitable approach to conflict management, especially if the party accommodating believes he is in the wrong or simply wants to increase goodwill with other parties to the conflict.

The **compromising** style occupies the center, with intermediate levels of cooperation and assertiveness. The "compromise" here is between pure competition and pure accommodation, and it is based on achieving a balance between personal and common interests. Often, this approach is labeled "distributed conflict management" because no one gets everything they want but a fraction of everyone's goals is nevertheless accomplished.[111] As with avoidance, this approach rarely makes an attempt to address or resolve the underlying sources of conflict but simply finds and chooses a way around them. Compromise is often applied to relational conflicts as a way of moving forward even though the underlying causes remain in place—the idea being that it is futile to try to "fix" people.

The **competitive** style, also known as the dominating or contending style, is in play when parties attempt to force their will, wishes, and perspectives on others, thereby creating competition between family members.

Competitively contending blocks others from achieving their goals. Typically, this provokes anger, stress, and distrust, which may lead to damaged relationships. The competitive style exhibits the characteristics of maximum assertiveness for one's own concerns and a minimum cooperativeness concerning another's. It is a zero-sum, win-lose conflict management strategy and may create adverse long-term outcomes in a family firm.

Can it be successful?

Contending succeeds when one party has all the power and simply does not care about long-term relationships. By definition, it is a short-term solution. In cases where the immediate situation is seen as sufficiently dangerous that control must be aggressively asserted, the risk of long-term damage may be worth taking.

In the **collaborative** style, both the assertiveness to satisfy one's own concerns and the cooperativeness to satisfy the other party's concerns are maximized. Also known as an integrating conflict management style, this strategy aims to create a mutually acceptable situation that accommodates all concerned parties in what is considered a win-win.

When the collaborative style is possible, its application increases team effectiveness, leads to solutions that satisfy all parties, and reduces the chance that underlying conflicts will re-emerge. The result is the satisfaction of the interests of both parties involved in the conflict.

With respect to the Big-5 factors discussed earlier in the book, a recent study showed that extroversion, conscientiousness, openness, and agreeableness all have a positive relationship with a collaborative (integrating) style. Extroversion also has a positive relationship with a competitive (dominating) style, while agreeableness and neuroticism have negative relationships with a competitive style. Extroversion, openness, and conscientiousness have a negative relationship with avoidance, while agreeableness and neuroticism have a positive relationship with avoidance.[112]

A recent study of the impact of the family firm leader's conflict management style on the business found that the collaborative style resulted in less conflict in the family and higher perceptions of stronger firm performance. The competition and avoidance conflict management styles were associated with higher levels of conflict and lower perceptions of family firm performance.[113]

Managing the Dispute through Third-Party Intervention

Effectively resolving a dispute requires three steps. First, parties must recognize that conflict has multiple sources, some of which, likely, have yet to be identified. Second, they must accurately diagnose the causes of the conflicts. Third, dispute resolution methods must be tailored to address the underlying sources.[114]

In the throes of a conflict, the family may want nothing more or less than to end that conflict. What must be remembered, however, is that conflicts have causes, and unless the underlying driving sources of a conflict are accurately diagnosed, addressed, and resolved, conflict is likely not only to persist, but to become more complicated, more intractable, and more damaging. It is important for the parties to acknowledge that there is no one best way to resolve a dispute, especially in complex matters such as family business disputes, and that the multiple aspects of the conflict may require multi-pronged dispute resolution strategies.

This is where third-party intervention can be invaluable. A counselor who specializes in mediating family business disputes not only plays the necessary role of a neutral referee but also applies an orderly process to addressing the conflict.

Defining the Client

Going into the dispute, the practitioner must shed the idea that the individual who created the business is the client. The reality here is that the "client" is the whole family relationship. Effectively, then, the advisor serves multiple clients, which may complicate matters but will prove much more effective when multiple perspectives matter. In the larger family enterprise system, where critical information is not kept in one subsystem or professional silo, the multiple-client mindset becomes even more critical. Practitioners must therefore learn to expand their definition of *client* in both a longitudinal and latitudinal fashion. They must expand their understanding of the family relationships longitudinally, over multiple generations, and they must also look latitudinally, at the growth of families to include in-laws (or, as many clients like to call them, out-laws).

For lawyers, who practice within the confines of conflicts rules and the codes of professional conduct, this broader conception of the client presents a unique retainer challenge. One way to address potential conflicts issues is to enter into a written agreement with the initial client, often the owner-founder, which explicitly permits communication and information-sharing with other family members and professionals working together as a multidisciplinary team. The more specific the information-sharing agreement, the better. This will assist in avoiding misunderstandings or difficulties that will only exacerbate conflict and the potential for conflict.

Building and Leading a Multi-Disciplinary Team

Advising family-owned businesses often brings together professionals from diverse disciplines, including lawyers, mediators, facilitators, accountants, family therapists, and management consultants. Advisors may work in one or more of the three principal family business subsystem domains (ownership, family, and business):

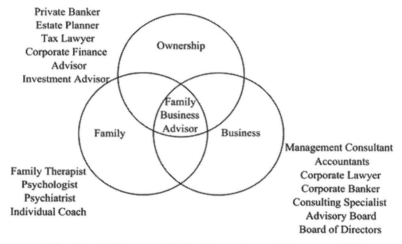

The Family Business Multi-Disciplinary Team Model[115]

Traditionally, family business professionals and advisors have invariably worked independently of one another, which meant that there was little opportunity to build a holistic picture of the family enterprise system and thus serve families more effectively. In fact, siloed independent advising often leads to the client receiving suboptimal, differing, or even conflicting advice from different advisors. To improve the quality and consistency of advice, researchers suggest that advisors from different disciplines work collaboratively so that all three subsystem domains figure in addressing the issues facing the family enterprise.[116]

Although working in multidisciplinary teams provides greater comprehension and coordination, especially in the conflict management process, this approach does present its own challenges. Consulting with multiple professionals is time-consuming and requires a strong commitment to managing the process of the team. Whether codified into a formal multidisciplinary charter or informally established, the team must be organized, coordinated, and facilitated by a single leader. In some cases, a practitioner who has developed the most enduring relationship with the business family may effectively "quarterback" a larger advisory team. By integrating advice in this way, the business family benefits from more effective and enduring conflict management assistance.

Information Gathering

Once the advisory team is put together and the retainer agreement concluded, information-gathering and an analysis of the family business conflict proceed. This process should provide a roadmap for selecting an appropriate conflict management strategy, which will also allow for the discovery of any possible discrepancies between the conflict as initially presented, or perceived conflict, and whatever underlying conflict may surface in the family firm system.[117]

- **Genogram:** The family genogram is a visual representation of the membership of a family, including relationships as well as exits and entries into the system. A genogram is an invaluable graphical means of organizing the mass of information that is gathered during a family assessment. It facilitates the identification of patterns in the family system, which makes for a more targeted analysis and assistance.[118]

Preparing a genogram starting from the founding generation can, from the start of the analysis, be a powerful tool to capture the family system's key players and relationships. Each row depicts a family generation and lists (from left to right) siblings from oldest to youngest. Using legends; gender, marital status, age, nature of relationships, and other details, such as role in the business and ownership, can be included. The genogram is helpful in itself to the business family and it serves the advisor as a means of understanding the dynamics of the family.

- **Personal Interviews and Document Review:** Personal interviews are indispensable in gathering information and building an understanding of the relationships and dynamics in the family business system. Advisors should interview the following eight categories of individuals:
  1. Non-family owners/investors: owners who are not family and not involved in the business.
  2. Family: members of the family who do not own or work in the business.
  3. Non-family managers and employees: non-family members who work in the business.
  4. Inactive family owners: family members who have ownership but who do not work in the business.
  5. Owner-managers: non-family members who have ownership and are active in the business.
  6. Family employees: family members who do not have ownership but who are active in the business.
  7. Family owner-managers: family owners who also work in the business.
  8. External stakeholders: customers and suppliers or other non-family owner stakeholders, advisors, lawyers, accountants, and other professionals involved.[119]

While information-gathering, through personal interview and document review, it is helpful to organize the information obtained by system circle.

With respect to the **family circle**, needed information includes family history, family roles and relationships, patterns and values, decision making, communication and conflict management styles.

In the **business circle**, organizational chart(s), any strategic or business plan(s), mission statements, systems, processes, leadership structure, finances, and the like should be gathered.

In the **ownership circle**, needed information includes legal documentation, the nature and distribution of ownership, the nature and organization of the board of directors, and the like.[120]

Overall, documents to be collected for review include financial statements, company constating (organizational) documents, shareholders' agreements, organizational charts, vision statements, mission statements, strategic plans, trust documents, and all related estate planning documentation, compensation policies, and similar materials.

Analysis: The Family Business Conflict Code Model

A conflict analysis model can help clarify complex systems and provide useful guidance to practitioners. As Bernard Mayer puts it in *The Dynamics of Conflict: A Guide to Engagement and Intervention*: "A framework for understanding conflict is an organizing lens that brings conflict into better focus. There are many different lenses we can use to look at conflict, and each of us will find some more amenable to our way of thinking than others ... We need frameworks that expand our thinking, that challenge our assumptions, and that are practical and readily usable."[121] The Family Business Conflict Code is a model of family business conflict that practitioners can use to diagnose family firm conflict as well as obtain guidance about what interventions may help and why:

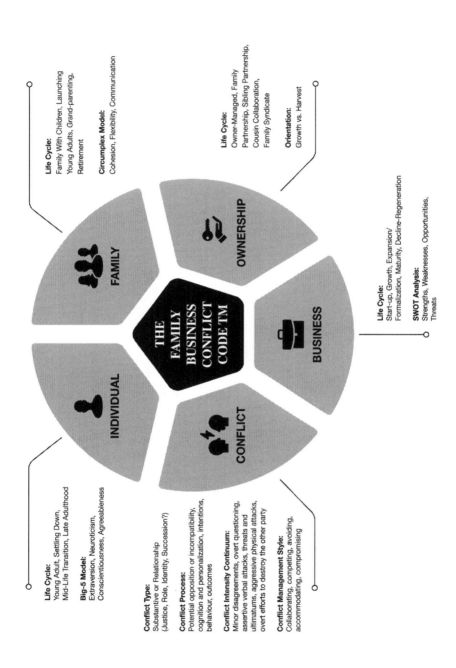

Life Cycle:
Family With Children, Launching
Young Adults, Grand-parenting,
Retirement

Circumplex Model:
Cohesion, Flexibility, Communication

Life Cycle:
Owner-Managed, Family
Partnership, Sibling Partnership,
Cousin Collaboration,
Family Syndicate

Orientation:
Growth vs. Harvest

Life Cycle:
Start-up, Growth, Expansion/
Formalization, Maturity, Decline-Regeneration

SWOT Analysis:
Strengths, Weaknesses, Opportunities,
Threats

Conflict Type:
Substantive or Relationship
(Justice, Role, Identity, Succession?)

Conflict Process:
Potential opposition or incompatibility,
cognition and personalization, intentions,
behaviour, outcomes

Conflict Intensity Continuum:
Minor disagreements, overt questioning,
assertive verbal attacks, threats and
ultimatums, aggressive physical attacks,
overt efforts to destroy the other party

Conflict Management Style:
Collaborating, competing, avoiding,
accommodating, compromising

Life Cycle:
Young Adult, Settling Down,
Mid-Life Transition, Late Adulthood

Big-5 Model:
Extraversion, Neuroticism,
Conscientiousness, Agreeableness

FAMILY

OWNERSHIP

THE FAMILY BUSINESS CONFLICT CODE TM

BUSINESS

CONFLICT

INDIVIDUAL

After completing the information-gathering phase, data can be mapped out and organized in each of the Individual, Family, Ownership, Business, and Conflict sections of the Conflict Code.

In the **Individual** section, a party can be mapped along the individual developmental cycle of young adult, settling down, mid-life transition, and late adulthood. In terms of individual personality traits that impact conflict, parties can be assessed with one of the various Big-5 personality tests to assess their propensity for conflict and projected conflict management styles. With the proviso that only a licensed mental health professional can diagnose an individual, the conflict resolution practitioner can use these results to form a working theory to aid in selecting an intervention.

In the **Family** section, a family can be allocated along the family life cycle of young family with children, launching young adults, grandparenting, and retirement. Self-reporting instruments, including FACES II and FACES III, can be used to assess a family along the continuums of cohesion and flexibility.[122] Family communication patterns can be assessed with such tools as the Family Communication Pattern (RFCP) instrument, which assesses constructive and destructive intrafamilial patterns of communication.[123]

In the **Ownership** section, the life cycle of owner-managed, family partnership, sibling partnership, cousin collaboration, and family syndicate can be assessed. Ownership types, and orientations toward either *growth* or *harvest* can be assessed as potential sources of conflict.

In the **Business** section, the business and industry life cycles can be assessed along the start-up, growth, expansion/ formalization, maturity, and decline-regeneration continuum. Assessments of the health of the business itself can be performed, including an analysis of strengths, weaknesses, opportunities, and threats (or SWOT analysis). Tools to assist with understanding the strengths and weaknesses of the family firm's capabilities and any opportunities and threats to it can highlight potential pressures and sources of conflict in that area of the family business system.[124]

In the **Conflict** section, the presenting conflict can be mapped by type: substantive or relationship. If the conflict appears to be relational, as it often is in family businesses, the usual suspects can be investigated first. These include justice, role, identity, and succession conflicts. They can be assessed along a continuum that pinpoints where they are in terms of process, intensity, and conflict management styles of the involved parties.

Based on the integrated analysis of the Family Business Conflict Code, the underlying sources of conflict can be determined, and appropriate strategies employed to address them. It may be that individual or family therapy should be employed. Governance structures such as a family charter or structured family meetings might be recommended to remedy family miscommunication and ambiguity. Documentation of ownership relationships using a shareholders' agreement may be indicated. The business may require such governance structures as a formalized and independent board of directors or a business plan to address business challenges.

Conflict Resolution Processes

Conflicts are almost always dynamic rather than static, with the potential for the source of conflict to change during attempts to resolve the initial dispute. Conflict resolution professionals must therefore remain attuned to the range of possible sources of conflict so that changes in the nature or sources of a given dispute can be identified promptly and addressed appropriately. The dynamic nature of disputes means that conflict management must be flexible to allow for variation in the dispute resolution method in order to match the changing nature or differing perceptions of the conflict sources.

One or more of the following conflict resolution processes may be part of a family business conflict management strategy:

Negotiation is any form of communication in which opposing parties discuss steps they might take to resolve a dispute between them. Negotiation can occur directly between the parties or indirectly through agents, such as lawyers, acting on behalf of the parties. Negotiation can be managed by a third party, such as a professional facilitator.

Mediation is a non-binding process in which a neutral, impartial third party with no decision-making authority attempts to facilitate an agreement between disputing parties. Mediation is generally a private dispute resolution process.

Conciliation can range from an approach that is essentially mediation with a more interventionist third party, to shuttle negotiations, in which the neutral third party "shuttles" between disputants who are unwilling to meet in person.

Joint fact-finding involves parties choosing a neutral fact-finder who investigates, reviews documents, and interviews witnesses to determine the facts in a dispute.

Neutral evaluation is a process in which parties obtain from an experienced (and possibly expert) neutral third party a non-binding reasoned evaluation of their case on its merits. The opinion or assessment is expected to have persuasive value, especially because the neutral third party is jointly selected.

Med-Arb, short for mediation-arbitration, is a process in which one person acts first as a mediator, then as an arbitrator. If the initial mediation is unsuccessful, the mediator becomes an arbitrator and makes a binding decision.

Arbitration is a conflict resolution process in which disputes are submitted to a neutral adjudicator through presentation of evidence and arguments. The arbitrator is empowered to render a legally binding decision. Arbitration is generally a private, voluntary method of adjudication, and a contract such as a shareholders' agreement may stipulate that disputes must be resolved by arbitration rather than litigation.

Adjudication refers to a dispute resolution process in which a neutral third party hears each party's evidence and arguments before rendering a decision that is binding on them. This includes arbitration and traditional litigation (for example, a trial).

Determining which dispute resolution process is right for a given business family at a given point in time in a given conflict is, of course, highly contextual and depends on many factors. Before choosing a conflict management process, it is important for practitioners and family members to assess, in a systematic way, the source of the conflict, the type of conflict at issue, the severity of the conflict, how the conflict could be resolved, and the possible benefits and risks of each potential conflict management process.

A preferred method of conflict resolution for a family firm lies in collaborative or cooperative forms of third-party intervention. If these approaches can resolve a conflict constructively, negative impacts will be minimized and the family firm and its performance may even be enhanced, emerging from the conflict better than they were before entering into the conflict. This type of resolution is more accurately called "transformation," and it is the subject of the final chapter.

CHAPTER 6

TRANSFORMATION

tronach. In Canada, the family name became shorthand for the mother of all family business conflicts. Recall how sensationally bad it was. In September 2018, rags-to-riches auto parts magnate Frank Stronach, an Austrian immigrant who founded a family enterprise that made him one of the giants of Canadian business, sued his daughter, two grandchildren, and non-family executive Alon Ossip for more than a half-billion dollars, alleging mismanagement, conspiracy, fraud, and document falsification all aimed at robbing him of his business. Daughter Belinda Stronach defended the suit by alleging that her father squandered vast sums on Quixotic passion projects. Citing hundreds of millions of dollars in losses, she countersued. As Ossip wrote in his defence, "[Frank Stronach's] refusal to let go of his failing business ventures has become financially disastrous."

Suddenly, on August 13, 2020, father and daughter issued a surprise joint statement. To the shock of Canadians who had been following the Stronach saga as a real-life soap opera, they had settled out of court:

"I am pleased that my father will be able to focus on an agricultural business and related projects that are his passion. The settlement will allow the Stronach Group to continue building successful companies with quality jobs that contribute to the community," Belinda said.

"I am glad that our disagreements have been resolved amongst ourselves and have utmost confidence in the Stronach Group's thoroughbred racing and gaming businesses, which will remain under Belinda's management," Frank said.[125]

An account in *The Canadian Press* commented almost disappointedly on the "cool but conciliatory tone," which stood in "stark contrast" to the fireworks of the lawsuits exchanged between the parties.[126] Yet given the magnitude of the difference between the state of the conflict when the suit and countersuit were filed— September 2018 and January 2019—and at the August 14, 2020 joint statement, we must recognize more than a change in "tone." What we see is a transformation.

Frank Stronach's suit and Belinda Stronach's defence and counterclaim, as discussed in Chapter 1, staked out in corrosive detail irreconcilable differences. Nothing was held back. Nothing was conceded.

"Resolution," in fact, did not appear to be an option. Recall what conflict expert John Lederach said about the downside of resolution: it carries "with it a danger of co-optation, an attempt to get rid of conflict when people [are] raising important and legitimate issues."[127] Now, Lederach is a Professor of International Peacebuilding at the University of Notre Dame and the founding director of the Center for Justice and Peacebuilding, headquartered at Eastern Mennonite University in Harrisonburg, Virginia. He specializes in negotiating conflicts between nations and, more often, between or among factions within a nation. One has only to think of such conflicts as the ongoing Israeli-Palestinian dispute to appreciate how the parties may see "resolution" as inevitably co-optation, cover-up, and, indeed, surrender. The prevailing mindset in Stronach, as in many other family business conflicts, resembled that of the Israeli-Palestinian dispute. Neither party could entertain even the dimmest glimmer of a middle ground called resolution.

Come August 2020, father and daughter summarily settled the matter by mutually abandoning the middle ground. They withdrew from court—the arena of the ultimate resolution, namely adjudication—and instead transformed their contention for the throne of a family business empire by decreeing *two* empires, each with its own throne. Frank and his wife, Elfriede, would assume ownership and control of a stallion and breeding business, as well as farm operations in North America, and all European assets. Daughter Belinda would remain chairwoman and president of the Stronach Group, which gave her control of its horse racing, gaming, real estate, and related assets.

There is, of course, no telling how durable the Stronach settlement will prove. But it was decidedly transformative in that, instead of attempting to mollify the parties with possession, say, of 50% each of a single thing, it transformed that thing into two things and (with apologies to Dr. Seuss) awarded 100% possession of Thing 1 to Frank and 100% possession of Thing 2 to Belinda. King Solomon famously proposed to resolve disputed possession of an infant by cleaving the baby in two. In Stronach, the parties chose the far less bloody course of transforming one baby into twins.

To repeat, we cannot at this point predict the fate of the settlement. Nor can we declare that it will certainly improve the collective performance of the business units now divided from one another. We can speculate, however.

With respect to performance, the transformation should prevent one set of businesses from bleeding money from the other. At the very least, this will make planning, investment, and management far easier, more efficient, and less ambiguous. With respect to the longevity of the settlement, we may note that the settlement transformed the object of the conflict from possession to control. We all want control in every aspect of life. Family conflicts often center around issues of control, business conflicts likewise. *Family* business conflicts? In these, the issue of control is fueled both by family dynamics and by business imperatives, and so assumes extraordinarily compelling power.

Savvy businesspeople appreciate ownership, but they understand that ownership does not necessarily confer control and control does not necessarily require ownership. More important, they understand that, of the two, ownership or control, control is far more desirable. By transforming the crux, the gravamen, of the conflict from ownership to control, the out-of-court Stronach settlement leveraged the power of family—the familiness advantage—to give each party 100% control over the conduct of the business units that the settlement allocated to them.

Whatever it accomplished financially, the settlement does seem to have enabled an emotional breakthrough for the family in relation to its enterprises. "I am pleased that my father will be able to focus on an agricultural business and related projects that are his passion," Belinda told the press, using emotional descriptors ("pleased" and "passion") and a family descriptor as well: "my father". Frank's language is also revealing, as he spoke of being "glad" and reinforced the importance of family cohesion by explaining that what made him "glad" was that the dispute was "resolved amongst ourselves"—by the family and within the family. With that, he also expressed "confidence" in the competence and leadership ability of his daughter.

Going Long

I like to think that the out-of-court settlement reached in Stronach is the best possible outcome of this infamous family business dispute. I like to think that it will improve the performance and profitability of the family's enterprises, as well as strengthen the family itself and promote healing among its members. Most of all, I am impressed that the family, after engaging in so much debilitating ugliness, chose to aim higher, to think beyond both win-lose and resolution, finding instead a settlement that gave all parties 100% of something material and 100% of something emotional.

As a practitioner in the areas of the family office and the management of family conflict, I can tell you that not every conflict can be resolved, let alone transformed. Sometimes, the best you can hope for is to tamp things down for a time and hope the conflict dies a natural death. Other times, resolution, however imperfect, is all the family wants and is all the family can imagine. And that is sufficient, if it keeps the family's business running and satisfies the family despite the discontents all families endure from time to time.

But practitioners and families alike should be aware that successful conflict management need not always end in resolution. It can lead instead to the more ambitious goal of transformation. At its most ambitious, as John Lederach explains, "*Transformation* provides a clear and important vision because it brings into focus the horizon toward which we journey—the building of healthy relationships, locally and globally." Readers of this book, of course, are interested in the most "local" of relationships, that among family members, especially those in the business family. But even though our scope is narrower and more modest than the political and sociological range of Lederach's diplomatic endeavours, the level of ambition is similar. In both cases, transformation "requires real change in our current ways of relating."[128]

Do we really want to go this far? Change our ways of relating? How about just resolving the conflict at hand?

Victoria Price, a twenty-eight-year-old TV news reporter in Tampa, Florida, received an email from a viewer: "Hi, just saw your news report. What concerned me is the lump on your neck. Please have your thyroid checked. Reminds me of my neck. Mine turned out to be cancer. Take care of yourself." She showed the email to her boyfriend, telling him she "didn't think the message was worth taking seriously." To her surprise, he reminded her that she had been complaining for a few months of feeling tired, and he advised her to have her doctor check it out. She followed his advice, was diagnosed with papillary thyroid cancer, and underwent surgery. "Victoria is lucky that this was detected sooner than later," her surgeon remarked.[129]

No one wants to find a lump, and, if found, the first impulse may be to ignore or deny it. But, as with any symptom, that lump should be regarded as a gift—a precious warning that something deeper is wrong and needs to be examined, confronted, and addressed.

Conflict is a lump, a symptom. The worst thing to do is to ignore or deny it. But taking steps to only resolve the conflict can be just as pernicious if by "resolve," what is meant is to suppress, to co-opt, to deny "important and legitimate issues" at the deeper roots of the visible conflict.

Lederach observes that "our tendency [is] to view conflict by focusing on the immediate 'presenting' problems." As a result of this myopic focus, we "give our energy to reducing anxiety and pain by looking for a solution to the presenting problems without seeing the bigger map of the conflict itself." He explains that what we need to do is to view conflict through three lenses:

> First, we need a lens to see the immediate situation. Second, we need a lens to see beyond the presenting problems toward the deeper

patterns of relationship, including the context in which the conflict finds expression. Third, we need a conceptual framework that holds these perspectives together, one that permits us to connect the presenting problems with the deeper relational patterns. Such a framework can provide an overall understanding of the conflict, while creating a platform to address both the presenting issues and the changes needed at the level of the deeper relational patterns. [130]

As an example, Lederach explains that his family sometimes argues over doing the dishes. "We can have some good fights" over this task, which "seem to come out of nowhere ..." The discontent family members focus on the immediate situation, a pile of dirty dishes, but the "energy evoked suggests something far deeper is at play." What is it?

We are negotiating the nature and quality of our relationship, our expectations of each other, our interpretations of our identity as individuals and as a family, our sense of self-worth and care for each other, and the nature of power and decision-making in our relationship. Yes, all that is in the pile of dirty dishes.[131]

Like the lump on the young reporter's neck, the pile of dirty dishes is a symptom. And that means it is a gift, or at least, an invitation to dig deeper rather than settle for "resolving" the immediate problem. "Conflict flows from life. ... rather than seeing conflict as a threat, we can understand it as providing opportunities to grow and to increase understanding of ourselves, of others, of our social structures,"[132] and, I would add, understanding of our family and our family business.

Does this mean that families and their advisors should disdain and reject resolution of the immediate "presenting" conflict?

Of course not. But never forget that a family business is an "infinite game," the object of which is not to win, but to perpetuate the game; to perpetuate the family and the family business and, in the process, continually strengthen and improve both. So, in aiming for and executing conflict resolution, reserve one lens for the long view. Do not see the resolution of a particular conflict as a permanent end state. Go long. Take the transformative view. See resolution as neither more nor less than a space in which the relationships within the family, within the business, and between the family and the business can continuously evolve, strengthen, and improve.

ENDNOTES

1   Barbara Shecter and Geoff Zochodine, "A Stronach Family Feud: How things fell apart between the patriarch and his heir apparent," *Financial Post* (October 12, 2018), https://financialpost.com/new s/a-stronach-family-feud-how-things-fell-apart-between-the-patri arch-and-his-heir-apparent.

2   Leah McLaren, "The $500-Million Family Feud," *Toronto Life* (June 17, 2019), https://torontolife.com/city/inside-500-millio n-family-feud/.

3   McLaren, https://torontolife.com/city/inside-500-million-famil y-feud/.

4   McLaren, https://torontolife.com/city/inside-500-million-famil y-feud/.

5   McLaren, https://torontolife.com/city/inside-500-million-famil y-feud/.

6   Leigh Raper, "The 110-Foot Pegasus Living it Up in South Florida," *Atlas Obscura* (April 8, 2016), https://www.atlasobscura.com/ articles/the-110foot-pegasus-living-it-up-in-south-florida.

7   John Paul Lederach, *The Little Book of Conflict Transformation* (N.p.: Good Books, n.d.), Chapter 1; Kindle ed.

8   Lederach, Chapter 1.

9   Lederach, Chapter 3.

10   John W. Budd, Alexander J. S. Colvin, and Dionne Pohler, "Advancing Dispute Resolution by Understanding the Sources of Conflict: Toward an Integrated Framework, *ILR Review* (August 6, 2019), https://journals.sagepub.com/doi/abs/10.1177/0019793919866817; Lederach, Chapter 3.

11 Budd et al, https://journals.sagepub.com/doi/abs/10.1177/0019793
919866817; M. Afzalur Rahim, "Toward a Theory of Managing
Organizational Conflict," *International Journal of Conflict
Management* (March 1, 2002), https://www.emerald.com/insight/
content/doi/10.1108/eb022874/full/html.

12 Dean Tjosvold, "Defining conflict and making choices about
its management: Lighting the dark side of organizational life,"
International Journal of Conflict Management (May 1, 2006),
https://www.emerald.com/insight/content/doi/10.1108/1044406
0610736585/full/html.

13 L. Pondy, "Organizational Conflict: Concepts and Models,"
Administrative Science Quarterly (1967), https://www.semanticscholar.
org/paper/Organizational-Conflict%3A-Concepts-and-Models-
Pondy/ac8ee8e0c5bab2c391597d36ab6056e845943277.

14 K. Jehn et al, "The Effects of Conflict Types, Dimensions, and
Emergent States on Group Outcomes," *Group Decision and
Negotiation* (2008), 17, 465; D. McKee et al, "Conflicts in Family
Firms: The Good and the Bad" in *The SAGE Handbook of Family
Business* (London: SAGE Publications Ltd., 2014), 514.

15 F. W. Kellermanns and K. A. Eddleston, "Feuding Families: When
Conflict Does a Family Firm Good," *Entrepreneurship Theory &
Practice* (2004), *28* (3), 209.

16 Jehn et al, 2008.

17 D. G. Pruitt, "Conflict, Escalation and De-escalation of., in D. J.
Christie, ed., *The Encyclopedia of Peace Psychology* (Malden, MA:
Wiley-Blackwell, 2011.

18 S. P. Robbins and T. Judge, *Organizational Behavior*, 15th ed.
(Boston, MA: Pearson, 2013).

19 Jehn et al, 2008.

20 P. J. D. Carnevale and A. M. Isen, "The influence of positive affect
and visual access on the discovery of integrative solutions in bilateral
negotiation," *Organizational Behavior and Human Decision Processes*
(1986), *37*(1), 1.

21 Robbins & Judge (1974)

22 B. Mayer, *The Dynamics of Conflict Resolution: A Practitioner's
Guide*, 1st ed. (San Francisco: Jossey-Bass, 2000.

23   Christopher Moore, *The Mediation Process: Practical Strategies for Resolving Conflict*, 4th ed. (San Francisco: Jossey-Bass, 2014).

24   P. Sharma, P., J. Chrisman, and K. Gersick, "25 Years of *Family Business Review*," *Family Business Review* (2012) *25*(1), 5-15; J. Halyk, *Research Matters in the Family Enterprise Field: Where Theory and Practise Meet* (Vancouver, BC: Sauder School of Business Business Families Centre, 2012); Grand Valley State University, Family Owned Business Institute, "Family Firm Facts,"

25   J. H. Astrachan, S. B. Klein, and K. X. Smyrnios, "The F-PEC Scale of Family Influence: A Proposal for Solving the Family Business Definition Problems," *Family Business Review* (2002) *15*(1), 45.

26   D. Miller et al. "Are family firms really superior performers? *Journal of Corporate Finance* (2007) *13*(5), 829; The Family Firm Institute, Inc., *Family Enterprise: Understanding Families in Business and Families of Wealth, + Online Assessment Tool* (Hoboken, NJ: Wiley, 2013); J. C. Carr and J. M. Sequeira, "Prior family business exposure as intergenerational influence and entrepreneurial intent: A Theory of Planned Behavior approach," *Journal of Business Research* (2007) *60*(10), 1090; A. M. Schuman, W. Sage-Hayward, and D. Ransburg, *Human Resources in the Family Business: Maximizing the Power of Your People*, 1st ed. (New York, NY: Palgrave Macmillan, 2015).

27   Graham F. Scott, "The 20 Biggest Family-run Businesses in Canada," *Canadian Business* (June 8, 2015), https://www.canadianbusiness.com/lists-and-rankings/richest-people/2015-family-business-ranking/.

28   Family Capital, "The Family 100 Influencers," https://www.famcap.com/the-worlds-750-biggest-family-businesses/.

29   Family Enterprise Xchange)2018).

30   Family Enterprise Xchange (2018)

31   M. Nordqvist and T. Zellweger, *Transgenerational Entrepreneurship: Exploring Growth and Performance in Family Firms Across Generations* (2010). Retrieved from http://www.alexandria.unisg.ch/Publikationen/54561.

32   E. J. Poza, *Family Business*, 3d ed. (Mason, OH: South-Western College Publishers, 2009). 9

33 A. Stewart and M. A. Hitt, "Why Can't a Family Business Be More Like a Nonfamily Business? Modes of Professionalization in Family Firms," *Family Business Review* (2012),*25*(1), 55.

34 M. Carney, et al. "Business Group Affiliation, Performance, Context, And Strategy: A Meta-Analysis," *The Academy of Management Journal* (2011), *54*(3), 437.

35 T. G. Habbershon and M. L. Williams, "A Resource-Based Framework for Assessing the Strategic Advantages of Family Firms," *Family Business Review* (1999), *12*(1), 1.

36 P. Berrone et al. "Socioemotional Wealth and Corporate Responses to Institutional Pressures: Do Family-Controlled Firms Pollute Less?" *Administrative Science Quarterly* (2010), *55*(1), 82-113.

37 W. G. Dyer and D. A. Whetten, "Family Firms and Social Responsibility: Preliminary Evidence from the S&P 500," *Entrepreneurship Theory and Practice* (2006), *30*(6), 785.

38 Bank of America and the Indiana University Lilly Family School of Philanthropy, "The 2018 U.S. Trust Study of High Net-Worth Philanthropy," https://www.privatebank.bankofamerica.com/artic les/2018-us-trust-study-of-high-net-worth-philanthropy.html.

39 Kirby Rosplock, "The Wealth Alignment Study Report of Findings," GenSpring Family Offices, 2008.

40 https://www.tata.com/business/tata-sons

41 D. L. Odom et al. "The most influential family business articles from 2006 to 2013 using five theoretical perspectives," in E. Memili and C. Dibrell, eds., *The Palgrave Handbook of Heterogeneity among Family Firms* (London: Palgrave MacMillan), 2018, pp. 41-67.

42 L. R. Gómez-Mejía et al. "Socioemotional Wealth and Business Risks in Family-controlled Firms: Evidence from Spanish Olive Oil Mills," *Administrative Science Quarterly* (2007), *52*(1), 106.

43 Peter Jaskiewicz and WilliamDyer, "Addressing the Elephant in the Room: Disentangling Family Heterogeneity to Advance Family Business Research," *Family Business Review* (2017), https:// www.semanticscholar.org/paper/Addressing-the-Elephant-in-the-Room%3A-Disentangling-Jaskiewicz-Dyer/692c0b5b322571a54 c9400bd5fe2c2f382acb9ae.

44 S. Kraus, R. Harms, and M. Fink, "Family Firm Research: Sketching a Research Field," *International Journal of Entrepreneurship and*

Innovation Management (2011), *13*, 32; H. Mensching, S. Kraus, and R. Bouncken, "Socioemotional Wealth in Family Firm Research–A Literature Review," *Journal of International Business and Economics* (2014), *14*, 165.

45 W. E. Deming, *The New Economics: For Industry, Government, Education.* (Cambridge MA: MIT Press, 2000).

46 Family Enterprise Exchange, 2018

47 R. Tagiuri and J. Davis, "Bivalent Attributes of the Family Firm," *Family Business Review* (1996), *9*(2), 199.

48 R. Tagiuri and J. Davis, "The family business model for good governance" (1982), *http://www.qualified-audit-partners.be/index.php?cont=672&lgn=3.*

49 John L. Ward, "The Special Role of Strategic Planning for Family Businesses," *Family Business Review* (June 1, 1988), https://doi.org/10.1111/j.1741-6248.1988.00105.x.

50 T. M. Zellweger, R. S. Nason, and M. Nordqvist, "From Longevity of Firms to Transgenerational Entrepreneurship of Families: Introducing Family Entrepreneurial Orientation," *Family Business Review* (2012), *25*(2), 136.

51 Zellweger et al (2012).

52 R. Williams and V. Preisser, *Preparing Heirs: Five Steps to a Successful Transition of Family Wealth and Values*, 1st ed. (San Francisco: Robert Reed Publishers, 2010), p. 16.

53 J. E. Hughes Jr., E. E. Massenzio, and K. Whitaker, *Complete Family Wealth*, 1st ed. (Hoboken, NJ: Bloomberg Press, 2017.

54 M. Nordqvist and T. Zellweger (2010); L. Hausner and D. K. K. Freeman, *The Legacy Family: The Definitive Guide to Creating a Successful Multigenerational Family* (New York: Palgrave Macmillan, 2009)..

55 J. E. Hughes Jr. et al (2017).

56 L. Hausner amd D. K. K. Freeman (2009).

57 J. E. Hughes Jr. et al (2017).

58 J. Carse, *Finite and Infinite Games* (New York: Free Press, 2013); S. Sinek, *The Infinite Game* (New York: Portfolio, 2019).

59 Karen A. Jehn and Elizabeth A. Mannix, "The Dynamic Nature of Conflict: A Longitudinal Study of Intergroup Conflict and Group

Performance," *The Academy of Management Journal* (April 2001), *44*(2), 238-251, https://www.jstor.org/stable/3069453?seq=1.

[60] A. C. Amason, "Distinguishing the Effects of Functional and Dysfunctional Conflict on Strategic Decision Making: Resolving a Paradox for Top Management Teams," *The Academy of Management Journal* (1996), *39*, 123-148, https://doi.org/10.2307/256633; Jehn 1997a, b; Jehn and Mannix (April 2001).

[61] Jehn 1997a.

[62] Amason (1996); A. C. Amason and D. M. Schweiger, "Resolving the paradox of conflict, strategic decision making, and organizational performance. *International Journal of Conflict Management* (1994), *5*(3), 239–253, https://doi.org/10.1108/eb022745; B. Brehmer, "Social judgment theory and the analysis of interpersonal conflict. *Psychological Bulletin* (1976), *83*(6), 985–1003, https://doi.org/10.1037/0033-2909.83.6.985; Carsten K. W. De Dreu and Annelies E. M. Van Vianen, "Managing relationship conflict and the effectiveness of organizational team," *Journal of Organizational Behavior* (April 20, 2001), https://onlinelibrary.wiley.com/doi/abs/10.1002/job.71.

[63] Wayne J. Irava and Ken Moores, "Clarifying the strategic advantage of familiness: Unbundling its dimensions and highlighting its paradoxes," *Journal of Family Business Strategy* (September 2010), *1*(3), 131-144.

[64] K. A. Eddleston and F. W. Kellermanns, "Destructive and productive family relationships: A stewardship theory perspective." *Journal of Business Venturing* (2007), *22*(4), 545; M. Deutsch, "Conflicts: Productive and Destructive," *Journal of Social Issues* (1969), *25*(1), 7; K. A. Jehn, "A Multimethod Examination of the Benefits and Detriments of Intragroup Conflict," *Administrative Science Quarterly* (1995), *40*(2), 256.

[65] S. M. Danes et al. "Predictors of Family Business Tensions and Goal Achievement," *Family Business Review* (1999), *12*(3), 241.

[66] Irena Knezevic, Kelly Bronson, and Chantal Clément, "What is (not) a family farm?" FLEdGE, https://fledgeresearch.ca/resources-results/food-growing-and-harvesting/what-is-not-a-family-farm/; United States Department of Agriculture, "Family Farms," https://nifa.

usda.gov/family-farms#:~:text=Family%20farms%20exclude%20 farms%20organized, farms%20in%20the%20United%20States.

67   Jonathan Small, "Family business and the 'familiness advantage,' *Progressive Dairyman Canada* (February 29, 2016), https://www. progressivedairycanada.com/topics/management/family-busines s-and-the-familiness-advantage.

68   P. T. Coleman and E. C. Marcus, *The Handbook of Conflict Resolution: Theory and Practice,* 3d ed. (San Francisco: Jossey-Bass, 2014.

69   T. Millon, *Disorders of Personality: DSM-IV and Beyond*, 2d ed. (New York: Wiley, 1995..

70   J. A. Davis et al, *Generation to Generation: Life Cycles of the Family Business* (Brighton, MA: Harvard Business Press, 1997)..

71   A. von Schlippe and K. A. Schneewind, "Theories from Family Psychology and Family Therapy, in *The SAGE Handbook of Family Business* (London: SAGE Publications Ltd., 2014).

72   K. E. Gersick, J. A. Davis, M. M. Hampton, and I. Lansberg, *Generation to Generation: Life Cycle of the Family Business* (Boston: Harvard Business School Press, 1997).

73   M. Gersteinand M. Papen-Daniel, *Understanding Adulthood. A Review and Analysis of the Works of Three Leading Authorities on the Stages and Crises in Adult Development, California Personnel and Guidance Association Monograph Number 15* (Fullerton CA: California Personnel and Guidance Association, 1981)..

74   J. Ward, *Keeping the Family Business Healthy—How to Plan for Continuing Growth, Profitability, and Family Leadership* (New York: Palgrave Macmillan, 2011).

75   K. de Vries, et al, *Family business on the couch. A psychological perspective* (Chichester, UK: John Wiley & Sons, 2007).

76   C. B. Broderick, *Understanding Family Process: Basics of Family Systems Theory* (Newbury Park, CA: SAGE Publications, Inc., 1993).

77   D. H. Olson, "Circumplex Model of Marital and Family Systems," *Journal of Family Therapy* (2000), *22*(2), 144.

78   J. G. Combs et al, "What Do We Know About Business Families? Setting the Stage for Leveraging Family Science Theories," *Family Business Review* (2019), doi:0894486519863508.

79   Olson (2000).

80   Olson (2000).

81 E. A. Paskewitz and S. J. Beck, "When Work and Family Merge: Understanding Intragroup Conflict Experiences in Family Farm Businesses," *Journal of Family Communication* (2017), *17*(4), 386.

82 P. T. Costa, R. R. McCrae, and G. G. Kay, "Persons, Places, and Personality: Career Assessment Using the Revised NEO Personality Inventory," *Journal of Career Assessment* (1995), *3*(2) 123..

83 O. P. John, R. W. Robins, and L. A. Pervin, *Handbook of Personality, Third Edition: Theory and Research* (New York: The Guilford Press, 2010).

84 Joyce E. Bono et al, "The Role of Personality in Task and Relationship Conflict," *Journal of Personality* (2002), *70*(3), 311.

85 P. T. Coleman, M. Deutsch, and E. C. Marcus, *The Handbook of Conflict Resolution: Theory and Practice,* 3d ed. (San Francisco, CA: Jossey-Bass, (2014).

86 Coleman et al (2014).

87 S. P. Kerr, W. R. Kerr, and T. Xu, "Personality Traits of Entrepreneurs: A Review of Recent Literature," *Foundations and Trends in Entrepreneurship* (2018), *14*(3), 279-356, http://dx.doi.org/10.1561/0300000080.

88 H. Zhao and S. Seibert, "The Big Five Personality Dimensions and Entrepreneurial Status: A Meta-Analytical Review," *The Journal of Applied Psychology* (2006), *91*, 259.

89 S. P. Kerr, W. R. Kerr, and T. Xu (2018).

90 D. Miller, "A Downside to the Entrepreneurial Personality? *Entrepreneurship Theory and Practice* (2015), *39*(1), 1.

91 Miller (2015).

92 Gary Johns and Alan M. Saks, *Oragnizational Behaviour: Understanding and Managing Life at Work,* 6th ed. (Tornoto: Pearson Canada, 2005).

93 John Lederach, *Little Book of Conflict Transformation: Clear Articulation of The Guiding Principles by a Pioneer in the Field.* (New York: Good Books, 2014), Chapter 1; Kindle Edition.

94 D. S. Medoza and J. L. Ward, *Family Business Governance: Maximizing Family and Business Potential.* (New York: Palgrave Macmillan, 2011).

95 J. H. Astrachan and K. S. McMillan, *Conflict and Communication in the Family Business. Marietta, GA: Family Enterprise Publishers,* 2003).

96   P. Leach and V. B. Mars, *Family Enterprises: The Essentials.* (London: Profile Books, 2016).

97   (Leach and Mars (2016); R. Arteaga and S. Menéndez-Requejo, "Family Constitution and Business Performance: Moderating Factors," *Family Business Review* (2017), 30(4), 320..

98   Harvard Business School, "Governing the Family-Run Business," *Harvard Business School: Working Knowledge* (2001). Retrieved from http://hbswk.hbs.edu/item/governing-the-family-run-business.

99   John A. Davis, "Governing the Family-Run Business," *Harvard Business School: Working Knowledge* (2001). *Retrieved from http:// hbswk.hbs.edu/item/governing-the-family-run-business.*

100   F. Neubauer and A. G. Lank, *The Family Business: Its Governance for Sustainability.* (New York: Routledge, 1998).)

101   John A. Davis et al, *Generation to Generation: Life Cycles of the Family Business* (Brighton, MA: Harvard Business Press, 1997).

102   C. Aronoff and J. Ward, *Family Business Ownership: How to Be an Effective Shareholder*, 2d. ed. (New York: Palgrave Macmillan, 2011).

103   M. E. Porter, *Competitive Strategy: Techniques for Analyzing Industries and Competitors*, 1st ed. (New York: Free Press, 1998)..

104   I. M. Kirzner, "Creativity and/or Alertness: a reconsideration of the Schumpeterian entrepreneur, in *The Driving Force of the Market* (New York, NY: Routledge, 2000)..

105   A. Cannella, "To Reap or to Sow? Governance, Strategy and Performance in Family Versus Founder Businesses (2007), PDF file retrieved from https://www.academia.edu/21487077/ To_Reap_or_to_Sow_Governance_Strategy_and_Performance_ in_Family_Versus_Founder_Businesses.

106   K. Rosplock, *The Complete Family Office Handbook* (Hoboken, NJ: John Wiley and Sons, Inc., 2014), pp. 10-14.

107   E. Su and J. Dou, "How Does Knowledge Sharing Among Advisors from Different Disciplines Affect the Quality of the Services Provided to the Family Business Client? An Investigation from the Family Business Advisor's Perspective," *Family Business Review* (2013), *26*(3), 256..

108   D. F. Womack, "Assessing the Thomas-Kilmann Conflict Mode Survey," *Management Communication Quarterly* (1988), *1*(3), 321..

109 S. P. Robbins and T. Judge, *Organizational Behavior*, 15ᵗʰ ed. (Boston: Pearson, 2013).

110 K. W. Thomas, "Conflict and Conflict Management: Reflections and Update, *Journal of Organizational Behavior* (1992), 13, 265-274, http://dx.doi.org/10.1002/job.4030130307.

111 R. L. Sorenson, "Conflict Management Strategies Used in Successful Family Businesses," *Family Business Review* (1999), *12*(2), 133..

112 D. Antonioni, "Relationship Between The Big Five Personality Factors And Conflict Management Styles," *International Journal of Conflict Management* (1998). Retrieved from https://www.emerald.com/insight/content/doi/10.1108/eb022814/full/html.)

113 Sorenson (1999).

114 J. W. Budd, A. J. S. Colvin, and D. Pohler, "Advancing Dispute Resolution by Understanding the Sources of Conflict: Toward an Integrated Framework," *ILR Review* (2019), https://doi.org/10.1177/0019793919866817.)

115 V. M. Strike, "Advising the Family Firm: Reviewing the Past to Build the Future," *Family Business Review* (2012), *25*(2), 156.

116 W. G. Dyer, "Potential Contributions of Organizational Behavior to the Study of Family-Owned Businesses," *Family Business Review* (1994), *7*(2), 109.

117 J. Hilburt-Davis and W. G. Dyer, *Consulting to Family Businesses: Contracting, Assessment, and Implementation,* 1ˢᵗ ed. (San Francisco: Pfeiffer, 2002).

118 M. McGoldrick, R. Gerson, and S. Petry, *Genograms: Assessment and Intervention,* 3d. ed. (New York: W. W. Norton, 2008).

119 (Hilburt-Davis and Dyer, (2002).

120 (Hilburt-Davis and Dyer (2002).

121 B. S. Mayer, *The Dynamics of Conflict: A Guide to Engagement and Intervention*, 2d ed. (San Francisco: Jossey-Bass, 2012), p. 4.

122 Edward F. Kouneski, *Family Assessment and the Circumplex Model: New Research Developments and Applications* (2000). PDF retrieved from http://citeseerx.ist.psu.edu/viewdoc/download?doi=10.1.1.195.3412&rep=rep1&type=pdf.

123 L. Ritchie and M. Fitzpatrick, "Family Communication Patterns: Measuring Intra-Personal Perceptions of Inter-Personal Relationships," *Communication Research* (1990), *17*.

124 Migrator, "SWOT, PESTLE and other models for strategic analysis (2011). Retrieved from https://www.nibusinessinfo.co.uk/content/swot-pestle-and-other-models-strategic-analysis.

125 The Canadian Press and AP, "Stronach family settles feud that divided founder Frank and daughter Belinda," *The Canadian Press* (August 13, 2020), https://www.nationalnewswatch.com/2020/08/13/stronach-family-settles-feud-that-divided-founder-frank-and-daughter-belinda/#.XzaH0uhKguU.

126 Canadian Press, https://www.nationalnewswatch.com/2020/08/13/stronach-family-settles-feud-that-divided-founder-frank-and-daughter-belinda/#.XzaH0uhKguU.

127 Lederach, chapter 1.

128 Lederach, chapter 1.

129 Cathy Free, "A TV reporter learned she had cancer after a viewer sent her a concerned email," *The Washington Post* (August 11, 2020), https://www.washingtonpost.com/lifestyle/2020/08/11/tv-reporter-learned-she-had-cancer-after-viewer-sent-her-concerned-email/.

130 Lederach, chapter 2.

131 Lederach, chapter 2.

132 Lederach, chapter 2.